A Sallust Reader

BC LATIN Readers

Series Editor:
Ronnie Ancona

These readers provide well annotated Latin selections written by experts in the field, to be used as authoritative introductions to Latin authors, genres, topics, or themes for intermediate or advanced college Latin study. Their relatively small size (covering 500–600 lines) makes them ideal to use in combination. Each volume includes a comprehensive introduction, bibliography for further reading, Latin text with notes at the back, and complete vocabulary. Nineteen volumes are currently scheduled for publication; others are under consideration. Check our website for updates: www.BOLCHAZY.com.

A Sallust Reader

Selections from *Bellum Catilinae,*
Bellum Iugurthinum,
and *Historiae*

Victoria E. Pagán

Bolchazy-Carducci Publishers, Inc.
Mundelein, Illinois USA

Series Editor: Ronnie Ancona
Volume Editor: Laurie Haight Keenan
Cover Design & Typography: Adam Phillip Velez
Map: Mapping Specialists, Inc.

A Sallust Reader
**Selections from *Bellum Catilinae, Bellum Iugurthinum,*
and *Historiae***

Victoria E. Pagán

Bolchazy-Carducci Publishers, Inc.
1570 Baskin Road
Mundelein, Illinois 60060
www.bolchazy.com

Printed in the United States of America
2009
by United Graphics

ISBN 978-0-86516-687-5

Library of Congress Cataloging-in-Publication Data

Sallust, 86-34 B.C.
 [Selections. 2009]
 A Sallust reader : selections from Bellum Catilinae, Bellum Iugurthinum, and Historiae /
Victoria E. Pagán.
    p. cm. -- (Latin readers)
 Includes bibliographical references and index.
 ISBN 978-0-86516-687-5 (pbk. : alk. paper) 1. Catiline, ca. 108-62 B.C. 2. Rome--
History--Conspiracy of Catiline, 65-62 B.C. 3. Jugurthine War, 111-105 B.C. 4. Rome--
History. I. Pagan, Victoria Emma, 1965- II. Sallust, 86-34 B.C. Bellum Catilinae. Selections.
III. Sallust, 86-34 B.C. Bellum Jugurthinum. Selections. IV. Sallust, 86-34 B.C. Historiae.
Selections. V. Title.
 PA6653.A2 2009
 937'.05--dc22

                                                                                              2009042979

Contents

List of Illustrations vii

Preface ix

Introduction xi

Latin Text 1

Bellum Catilinae

    3.3–4.5 1

    5.1–8 2

    15 3

    22 3

    23–24 4

    25 5

    27.2–29 5

    40–41 7

    53–54 8

    60–61 10

Bellum Iugurthinum

    6–7 12

    17–19 13

    84 16

    85 17

    86.1–3 22

Historiae

    2.70 23

Commentary 25

Bellum Catilinae

Sallust (re)turns to history, 3.3–4.5 25

The character of Catiline, 5.1–8 30

Catiline's sordid past, 15 33

Alleged human sacrifice, 22 36

Cicero learns of the conspiracy, 23–24 38

The portrait of Sempronia, 25 43

Catiline at Rome, Manlius in Etruria, 27.2–29 46

The Allobroges, 40–41 51

Cato and Caesar, 53–54 56

Catiline's last stand, 60–61 61

Bellum Iugurthinum

The character of Jugurtha, 6–7 67

The African excursus, 17–19 74

Marius prepares for campaign, 84 86

The speech of Marius, 85 91

Marius enlists soldiers, 86.1–3 112

Historiae

The banquet of Metellus, 2.70 115

Illustration Credits 119

Appendices

A: Timeline 121

B: Map: Rome and the Mediterranean in the
Late Republic 125

Vocabulary 127

List of Illustrations

(Including Maps)

1. Map of Rome, Showing the Location of the
    Gardens of Sallust xiv

2. Bust of Lucius Cornelius Sulla xvii

3. Bust of Marcus Tullius Cicero xix

4. Cicero Denouncing Catiline .xxi

5. Statue of Gaius Sallustius Crispus xxxix

6. Map of Rome and the Mediterranean in the
    Late Republic. 126

Preface

The more I read Sallust, the more I am amazed at the clarity of his intellect, and I shall have succeeded in this book if I convey even a fraction of the brilliance of his language and the excitement it evokes. The pleasure of reading Sallust is, to my mind, derived in large part from the simplicity of resolution, that is, from the simple ways he completes complex syntactical expectations. Then, upon reflection, one is struck by the frightfully honest content of his thought: the stark condemnation of moral decline, regardless of its origin; the incisive explanations for individual behavior, whether psychological or sociological; the ingenuous transparency of his self-presentation that engenders sincerity even as it begs skepticism.

The Latin text was meticulously prepared by Christopher McHale. As a lifelong student of Allen and Greenough's *New Latin Grammar* (Boston 1903, reprint), I consulted it exclusively. I prepared the vocabulary using the *Oxford Latin Dictionary* edited by P. G. W. Glare (Oxford 1985, reprint). I copied the precise subdefinition for a term when the particular passage of Sallust was cited. The brief Anglophone bibliography is intended as a starting point for further inquiry into specific topics, and the items are cited by author and year at appropriate places in the introduction and commentary. For students who wish to read the works of Sallust in their entirety, I highly recommend the commentaries by Ramsey (on the *Bellum Catilinae*), Comber and Balmaceda (on the *Bellum Iugurthinum*) and McGushin (on the *Historiae*), listed in the bibliography.

I thank the series editor Ronnie Ancona, Laurie Haight Keenan and the production staff at Bolchazy-Carducci, and the two anonymous readers for all of their assistance. The timely completion of this project was made possible by the Waldo W. Neikirk Term Professorship in the College of Liberal Arts and Sciences at the

University of Florida; for their steadfast and generous support, I thank Robert Wagman and Allan Burns. For patiently enduring the roughest of drafts, I sincerely thank Todd Bohlander, Gale Stone, Andrew Wolpert, and most especially Susanna Braund. For answering queries large and small within a matter of hours, if not minutes, I thank Tony Woodman, whose award-winning translation of the works of Sallust is a great boon to students and teachers alike. For their curiosity and keen eyes, I thank my students who bravely piloted the manuscript in Autumn 2008: Elizabeth Barnes, Salvatore Bartoloma, Shawn Bivins, Laura Burgher, Justin Byrd, Jennifer Cantleberry, Madison Dickinson, Robert Goddard, Sean Hill, Michael Jean, Bob Lotfinia, Jason Schatz, Harrison Sepulveda, Haley Smith, Megan Wallis, and Brian Wells. I learned the most from Brenda Fields, student of Sallust nonpareil.

My deepest gratitude belongs, again, to my husband Andrew Wolpert for his kindness and integrity, and to our children Abraham and Ellie for their flexibility and good cheer. I drafted this book under the cool shade of the oak tree at my grandparents' farmhouse in Ravenna, Ohio, and I dedicate it with love to my mother, Marjorie Sprott Pagán, an accomplished musician whose high school Latin teacher still attends her piano recitals.

VICTORIA EMMA PAGÁN
Coventry, Gainesville, Florida

Introduction

The austere and reserved historian Tacitus rarely uses superlatives, so when he calls Sallust "the most brilliant author of Roman history," (*Annals* 3.30.2), his praise must be deliberate. Quintilian, Rome's first endowed professor of rhetoric, speaks of "Sallustian brevity, than which nothing can be more perfect" (*Institutes of Oratory* 10.1.32). These are the opinions of men who were born more than a hundred years after Sallust. Theodor Mommsen, Nobel laureate and one of the greatest classical scholars of the nineteenth century, calls Sallust's *Bellum Iugurthinum* "fascinating and clever" (*The History of Rome*, vol. 3 p. 153). The reader who picks up Sallust is in good hands, by standards both ancient and modern.

∾ *Sallust's life and times*

Gaius Sallustius Crispus, or Sallust as we call him, was born in Amiternum, a Sabine town in the Apennine mountains about fifty miles northeast of Rome in 86 (see map; all dates are BCE). We know nothing of his childhood, but it is likely that he was educated at Rome. He tells us that he was a politically ambitious young man, but because he was the first in his family to pursue a career in politics, he could not rely on family connections; rather, his position was contingent upon his association with powerful men of rank and means. Therefore, the vicissitudes of his career depended on the men with whom he allied himself. The story of Sallust's political career is thus the story of the crumbling Republic.

If we assume that Sallust followed the *cursus honorum*, the ascending order of public office, then he was probably elected quaestor (treasurer) in 56 or 55; the quaestorship was the first rung on the career ladder, commonly held at the age of 27 to 30. We know for certain that Sallust was elected one of the tribunes of the plebs (officers of the people); within their legislative scope, tribunes of the plebs possessed the right to veto any act performed by another magistrate, a right that gave the office great revolutionary potential. Sallust was one of the tribunes in 52, a turbulent year that opened without consuls (two annually elected highest civil and military magistrates of Rome during the Republic). Three candidates vied for that office. Annius Milo was supported by aristocrats who wanted to preserve the authority of the Senate. Caecilius Metellus Scipio and Plautius Hypsaeus were supported by both Gnaeus Pompeius Magnus (Pompey the Great) and Publius Clodius Pulcher, who was running for praetor (second to the consuls, and chief of the judicial system). On January 18, Clodius was murdered on the Appian Way by a band of Milo's supporters. When Clodius' body was brought to the city and displayed in the Forum, the tribunes of the plebs—Sallust among them—incited riots, and the mob set fire to the Curia (the Senate House). A state of emergency was declared, and by February 25, Pompey was made sole consul; Milo was prosecuted, convicted, and sent into exile.

Tribunes of the plebs were immune from prosecution until their term of office expired, and as far as we can tell Sallust managed to avoid blame for any part he may have had in inciting the riots. Someone (perhaps Pompey?) must have been watching over him. Two years later, however, Sallust was expelled from the Senate by Appius Claudius Pulcher, one of the censors. Two censors were elected every four or five years, to hold office for eighteen months. As the seniormost elected magistrates in the *cursus honorum*, their primary function was to maintain the official register of citizens, but they also scrutinized the moral conduct of the citizens; a man whose conduct was reprehensible was disfranchised and obliged to pay taxes. The nominal charges against Sallust would have been either political or moral misconduct, but it is likely that his expulsion was in revenge for Milo's downfall. Due perhaps to the intervention of Julius Caesar, Sallust regained his seat in the Senate in 49.

By 49, Caesar dominated the political scene. He had held the consulship in the year 59, followed by his extraordinary governorship of the province of Cisalpine Gaul. Between the years 58 and 50, Caesar defeated numerous Gallic tribes and went so far as to invade the island of Britain. In his absence from Rome, his rival Pompey managed to enact a series of legislation designed both to hinder Caesar from returning to Rome without indemnity and to force him to lay down his troops. By 49, all diplomacy failed and Caesar had no choice but to march troops across the Rubicon, effectively invading Italy and inaugurating dictatorship.

Caesar then gave Sallust a series of military assignments in the civil war against Pompey. In 49, Sallust was sent to rescue the army of Gaius Antonius whom the Pompeians blockaded on the island of Curicta in the Adriatic. In 48, he was given command of a legion in Illyricum to clean up the remnants of Pompey's army that scattered after the defeat at Pharsalus. In 47, as praetor-elect, he was sent to quell a mutiny of Caesar's soldiers in Campania. In all three missions, Sallust failed. It would seem that Caesar's confidence in Sallust's ability was misplaced, but in 46, Sallust finally proved his worth. As praetor, Sallust accompanied Caesar on the African campaign that ended with the defeat of the remaining Pompeians at Thapsus. Sallust succeeded in capturing enemy supplies on the island of Cercina, off the coast of Roman Africa, and Caesar rewarded him with the governorship of the newly created province of Africa Nova, carved out of part of the Numidian kingdom (see map).

When Sallust returned to Rome in 45 as a wealthy man, he was accused of provincial maladministration, a charge routinely leveled against governors upon their return to Rome. It is likely that Caesar shielded him from prosecution (see Allen 1954); however, when Caesar was assassinated in 44, Sallust lost political protection and guarantee. Realizing his vulnerability, he retired from politics. Using the wealth he amassed and retained from Africa, he built a luxurious pleasure garden just beyond the *pomerium* (the formal boundary of the city of Rome) on a hill north of the Quirinal Hill, overlooking the Campus Martius (see Hartswick 2004). The *Horti Sallustiani* would have been legacy enough, for they were acquired by the emperor Nero and maintained for centuries by the emperors until Rome was sacked by the Goths in 410 CE. When Cardinal Ludovisi (the nephew of Pope Gregory XV) purchased the site in the early seventeenth century, he discovered some famous Roman

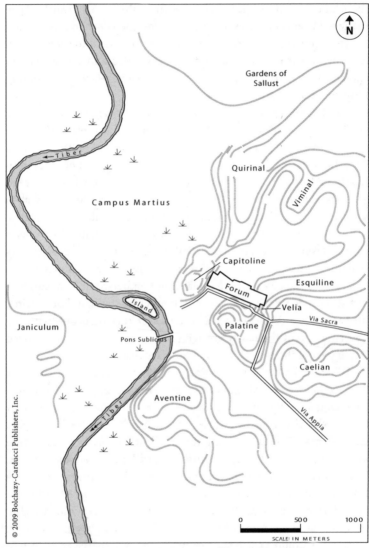

Fig. 1. Rome, Showing the Location of the Gardens of Sallust.

sculptures in this old garden, including *The Dying Gaul* and *The Suicidal Gaul and Wife*. But Sallust was destined to leave more than the shady respite of his gardens as a repository for an art collection. Since he would not stoop to hunt or farm, he spent his retirement writing history until his death, probably in the year 35, some four years before the battle of Actium.

From the sidelines, Sallust witnessed a remarkable decade in Roman history. The assassination of Caesar left political chaos in its wake. Political survival in the aftermath required a threefold combination of shrewdness, talent, and brute force. Marcus Antonius (Mark Antony), Caesar's fellow consul, immediately harnessed the power of public opinion for his own benefit by condemning the assassins Marcus Junius Brutus and Gaius Cassius Longinus. Caesar had adopted his great-nephew, Gaius Julius Caesar Octavianus, who inherited Caesar's estate and political influence. Marcus Aemilius Lepidus, who served as Caesar's *magister equitum* (major deputy) during the dictatorship, was quick to side with Mark Antony. In November 43, the *Lex Titia* established the triumvirate. Mark Antony, Octavian, and Lepidus divided up the provinces and were called *tresuiri rei publicae constituendae*, triumvirs for the establishment of the state. Rather than exercise the clemency of Caesar, who strategically pardoned his political enemies, they decided to root out their enemies by proscription, a list of Roman citizens who were declared outlaws and whose goods were confiscated. This tactic had not been employed since the ruthless dictatorship of Sulla in 82 (on the domination of Sulla, see below). The triumvirs condemned to death perhaps as many as 300 senators and 2,000 knights; Cicero topped the list and was hunted down and killed immediately. The triumvirs were particularly ruthless toward family and friends, as if they were trying to prove their loyalty to one another as much as drive out their political enemies.

After Brutus and Cassius were defeated at Philippi in 42, Mark Antony commanded the eastern provinces and Octavian the western. This division was reconfirmed in 40 and the alliance strengthened by the marriage of Antony and Octavia, Octavian's sister. Yet by 37, Antony had abandoned his wife to live openly with Cleopatra, the powerful Queen of Egypt, and he led a disastrous expedition to Parthia. At the same time, Lepidus, after a rash bid to displace Octavian, was forced to lay down his arms. Octavian, on the other hand, with the help of his talented friend Marcus Vipsanius Agrippa, managed to defeat the remnants of Pompey's supporters, led by Sextus Pompey, in 36. Caesar's heir was on the rise.

When Sallust died, the triumvirate was unraveling, but there was no telling how things would end up. In this political climate of change and uncertainty, Sallust produced history (for a recent study of the period and its effects on literature, see Osgood 2006).

⟨∿⟩ Sallust's texts and contexts

Between the years 44 and 35, Sallust wrote three works. The *Bellum Catilinae* (abbreviated *BC*) was published possibly in 42. Next he wrote the *Bellum Iugurthinum* (abbreviated *BI*), certainly finished by 39. He died in 35 before he finished the *Historiae*. Although these works treat specifically the conspiracy of Catiline in 63, the war against Jugurtha waged between 112 and 104, and the history of the Republic from 78 to 67 (so far as the fragments attest), nevertheless one major historical event casts a long and inescapable shadow across all three: the dictatorship of Sulla. More than forty times, Sallust mentions Sulla and attributes causes and effects to the dictatorship, its aftermath, and the fate of his veteran soldiers. Clearly for Sallust, the dictatorship was a defining moment in Roman history.

Lucius Cornelius Sulla Felix was born in 138. When Marius was waging the war against Jugurtha, Sulla was his quaestor in 107. By clever diplomacy he was able to secure the surrender of Jugurtha. He then served as a general for Marius against the Germans (104–103). By 97, he was elected to the praetorship, followed by a governorship of Cilicia, where he stayed until 92. When he returned to Rome in 91, he again served as a general, leading his army to numerous victories during the Social War (the conflict between Rome and her Italian allies that was eventually settled by the granting of citizenship). In 88 he was elected consul and given command of the army against Mithridates VI, king of Pontus. When this command was revoked by the

Fig. 2. Bust of Lucius Cornelius Sulla. Munich Glyptothek.

machinations of Marius, who feared his ascendancy, Sulla and six loyal legions marched on Rome. For the first time, a general crossed the *pomerium* with an army. Marius fled to a colony of his veterans in Africa, with whose support he returned to sack Ostia (the port of Rome); he was to take up the consulship in 86, but he died before he could take office. Ignoring the summons to stand for trial, Sulla left Rome to campaign in Greece for five years.

Upon his return, Sulla determined to regain control of Rome and marched again on the city in 82. Once in power, he posted lists of names of men with prices on their heads and extended his reign of terror for more than a year; the total number of victims of Sulla's proscriptions amounted to several thousands, most of them members of the equestrian order. The Senate, desperate for a return to normalcy and the rule of law, appointed him *dictator legibus faciendis et rei publicae constituendae causa*, "dictator for the making of laws and establishing the constitution." His reforms were aimed at returning control to the Senate, which he increased from 300 to 600 members; he also increased the number of quaestors and praetors, regulated the courts, and reduced the power of the tribunes of the plebs (on Sulla's reforms, see Gruen 1974, 6–46). In 79, Sulla resigned his dictatorship and retired to the Bay of Naples where he wrote his memoirs before he died of a chronic illness.

Because Sulla was instrumental in the capture of Jugurtha, Sallust devotes an entire paragraph to Sulla's character: "Since the subject reminds me of such a great man, it has seemed suitable to speak about his nature and habit in a few words" (*BI* 95.2). In the *Bellum Catilinae*, on the other hand, though Sulla is long dead, his influence is pervasive. His veterans were settled on property in Campania and Etruria confiscated by means of proscription; their numbers and their tenuous claim on the land constituted a menacing and volatile threat to the stability of Rome, and Sallust often returns to the theme of civil unrest caused by the violent displacement of citizens. For instance, in this volume's selections, we shall read that, "Meanwhile in Etruria, Manlius was inciting the common folk, eager for revolution because of their poverty and because of the resentment of insult, since during the reign of Sulla they had lost their land and all their possessions" (*BC* 28.4). Elsewhere Sallust describes the sort of people who were willing to join the Catilinarian conspiracy: "those whose parents had been proscribed in the victory of Sulla, their goods confiscated, their right to liberty stripped" (*BC* 37.9). By choosing to begin the *Historiae* with the year 78—after the death of Sulla—Sallust deliberately picks up where his predecessor Sisenna left off (on Sisenna, see below, p. xxix) and pointedly avoids having to narrate anything about the dictatorship directly. Sulla is conspicuous by his absence.

∾ *BELLUM CATILINAE*

In the year 66, the consuls-elect, Publius Cornelius Sulla and Publius Autronius, were charged with electoral bribery and disqualified from office. A second election was held, for which Lucius Sergius Catilina (Catiline) offered himself as candidate. But his application was rejected on the grounds that he had not yet been tried for the maladministration of his governorship of Africa the year before. Aurelius Cotta and Manlius Torquatus were elected consuls. Catiline stood again for election in 64; the other can-

Fig. 3. Bust of Marcus Tullius Cicero. Capitoline Museum, Rome, Italy.

didates were Cicero and Antonius. Cicero beat Catiline; apparently the stalwart oligarchy preferred to admit a newcomer to office than to abide the debt-ridden Catiline (Cicero was a *nouus homo*, the first in his family to become consul). In the summer of 63, when elections for the following year were held, Catiline stood again for the consulship, on a platform of debt cancellation—a promise one hardly imagines the Roman elite sanctioning. He was again defeated, this time by Decimus Junius Silanus and Lucius Licinius Murena, when he finally turned to force to achieve his ends.

With a band of dissatisfied men, Catiline formed a conspiracy. On October 18, an anonymous letter threatening bloodshed was brought to Cicero; the Senate proclaimed a state of emergency and by October 21 passed a decree known as a *senatus consultum ultimum,* giving full powers to the consuls to deal with the extraordinary threat to the Republic (in this volume's selections we read the provisions of the decree at *BC* 29.3). Catiline was planning a series of insurrections throughout Italy to coincide with organized arson in Rome. He intended to march on the city on the appointed day (October 27) with an army from Etruria led by Gaius Manlius. Cicero mobilized troops but lacked sufficient evidence to bring Catiline to justice.

On November 6, the conspirators met at the house of Marcus Porcius Laeca on the Street of the Scythemakers to delegate tasks and finalize their plans. Catiline instructed two of the conspirators to call on Cicero the next morning on the pretense of paying their respects and to murder him unsuspecting. Cicero found out about the plot through a deep-cover agent named Fulvia, a steady courtesan of one of the conspirators named Quintus Curius.

Armed with this knowledge, Cicero denounced Catiline in the Senate on November 7, in his first Catilinarian oration. The next day, Catiline left Rome to muster his forces in Etruria, and Cicero revealed the conspiracy to the people in his second Catilinarian oration. In Catiline's absence, the zealous conspirators enlisted the aid of the Allobroges, a Gallic tribe, but they betrayed the conspiracy to Cicero. Cicero seized the ringleaders at the Mulvian Bridge on December 2 and disclosed the entire affair, complete with witnesses and documentation, to the Senate on December 3. That afternoon Cicero addressed the people in the third Catilinarian oration to proclaim the revelation of the conspiracy and the salvation of the state.

Two days later the Senate debated the punishment of the conspirators and Cicero delivered his fourth speech against Catiline. Decimus Brutus (former consul in 62) proposed exile and confiscation of property. Julius Caesar (who was in 63 pontifex maximus, chief priest of Rome) argued forcefully that the five prisoners not be executed; however, convinced by Marcus Porcius Cato (a former quaestor and tribune of the plebs elect), the Senate consented to their immediate execution. Cicero himself escorted the conspirator Lentulus from the aedile's house on the Palatine hill, along the Via Sacra, across the forum, to the so-called Tullianum, the prison where the other four conspirators were waiting. The five were promptly executed. The consequences of this action would dog Cicero for the rest of his life (see Habicht 1990).

Fig. 4. Cicero Denouncing Catiline. Cesare Maccari (1840–1919).
Wallpainting, Palazzo Madama, Rome, Italy.

In 61, Cicero had given damaging evidence against Clodius Pulcher, who was on trial for trespassing on the Bona Dea festival disguised as a woman. Clodius never forgot this slight, and in 58 he took his revenge. As one of the tribunes of the plebs, he introduced a bill that anyone who executed a citizen without a trial should be banished. Cicero left Rome before he could be convicted. Clodius then passed a second law declaring Cicero an exile and destroyed Cicero's house on the Palatine Hill. In 57, Cicero was recalled by a law of the people. In spite of his continued political activity, Cicero never recovered his former standing. After the assassination of Caesar in 44, Cicero proclaimed openly that Antony should have been killed too. In a series of speeches known as the *Philippics*, Cicero tried to have Antony declared a public enemy, but to no avail. When Antony and Octavian joined forces in 43, Antony put Cicero's name on the list of citizens to be hunted down and murdered, and Octavian did not object. Cicero was killed on 7 December 43, twenty years and two days after the execution of the Catilinarian conspirators. The *Bellum Catilinae*, published the next year, was written in the shadow of these grisly events.

∾ *BELLUM IUGURTHINUM*

Sallust's second monograph is a more ambitious undertaking than the first. The *Bellum Catilinae* deals primarily with events of the year 63 in the city of Rome and nearby towns. The *Bellum Iugurthinum*, on the other hand, covers a seven-year period with events that take place on two continents. The second monograph is twice as long as the first and its subject matter more complicated, though as Kraus 1999 demonstrates, the sense of disorder in the *Bellum Iugurthinum* is a carefully contrived narrative strategy.

At the end of the Second Punic War (218–201), the Romans handed over Numidian territory to King Masinissa, who ruled for sixty years. He united the nomadic tribes from Mauritania in the west to Cyrenaica in the east. When he died in 148, he left this vast Numidian kingdom under the protection of the Romans. Scipio Aemilianus divided rule among Masinissa's three sons, Micipsa, Gulussa, and Mastanabal, the father of an illegitimate son named Jugurtha. Gulussa and Mastanabal died, leaving Micipsa sole heir. Micipsa had two sons of his own, Adherbal and Hiempsal. According to Sallust, Jugurtha's strength and charisma alarmed Micipsa, who feared for his and his sons' position. In an attempt to rid himself of this threatening illegitimate nephew, Micipsa sent Jugurtha to help Scipio Aemilianus with operations in Spain; however, the plan failed and Jugurtha only proved himself the more competent in war and capable of securing popular favor. Micipsa had no choice but to adopt Jugurtha and bestow on him equal rights with his sons.

When Micipsa died in 118, Jugurtha wasted no time in consolidating his power (though for a reminder that such a description of a power-hungry Jugurtha is the result of a one-sided, Roman-authored narrative, see Claassen 1993). In 117, Hiempsal was assassinated and Adherbal defeated and driven out of Africa; he fled to Rome for protection. The Senate partitioned Numidia between Jugurtha and Adherbal, but Jugurtha continued to attack his stepbrother. Unsuccessful embassies from Rome failed to mediate the conflict, and in 112 Jugurtha was finally able to corner Adherbal and besiege him at Cirta, an important center of grain trade. When the city fell,

Jugurtha ruthlessly murdered Adherbal and many Italian merchants who resided in Cirta (for a careful study of the episode, see Morstein-Marx 2000). The Senate declared war on Jugurtha.

The war was waged in three phases, each lasting about two years. In the years 112–110, the consuls Calpurnius Bestia and then Spurius Albinus were sent in succession against Jugurtha. Bestia attempted a settlement with Jugurtha, but negotiations failed. Spurius Albinus, anxious to campaign for office, left his (incompetent) brother Aulus in command of the troops in Africa, but Aulus was forced to capitulate in a disastrous surrender. Albinus attempted to rehabilitate his reputation, but his army was too demoralized to take up battle.

In 109, the consul Quintus Caecilius Metellus (later he will earn the honorary name Numidicus) took command of the forces in Africa. His first order of business was to re-establish discipline in the army. Unlike Bestia and Albinus, Metellus was an astute diplomat and a shrewd opponent. Metellus was able to besiege Jugurtha's stronghold at Zama, and in spite of fierce battle the town was finally abandoned. During the winter months, Metellus attempted to bribe Bomilcar, Jugurtha's right-hand man; however, at the last minute Bomilcar balked and the plot failed. Jugurtha executed Bomilcar and escaped with his life and enough treasure to support himself in extended flight. Yet when he could no longer pay his Gaetulian mercenaries, Jugurtha then enlisted his father-in-law Bocchus, King of Mauritania, in the struggle against the Romans. In 108, while Metellus occupied Cirta, he learned that his lieutenant Gaius Marius had been elected consul. Diplomacy with Bocchus failed; Metellus was sent home.

In 107, Marius entered the consulship and the final phase of the war began. He managed to capture Capsa and to reduce Numidian strongholds across the country as far as a fortress near the River Muluccha, some seven hundred miles to the west on the Moroccan frontier. In the midst of these stunning victories, the quaestor Sulla arrived with the cavalry Marius desperately needed and the noble birth he sorely lacked. Sulla was able to convince Bocchus to betray Jugurtha, who was exhibited in Marius' triumphal parade. Jugurtha was imprisoned in the Tullianum and executed by the Romans in 104.

The abrupt ending of the monograph suggests a self-conscious incompleteness (see Levene 1992) and a deliberate acknowledgment of the Jugurthine war as but one episode in the long history of Rome.

Marius emerges as a brilliant and talented tactician, but his most important contribution was his reform of the Roman army. First, he updated equipment. All ranks were outfitted with the javelin and sword in order to duel in a cut-and-thrust technique borrowed from the gladiatorial schools. Second, he revised the organization of the army. The cohort, ten to a legion, became the standard unit, and the number of officers per legion was increased to sixty. Third, Marius made the entire army more mobile by making the men carry their own equipment. Hence his soldiers became known as "Marius' mules." But perhaps most importantly of all the reforms, Marius converted the Roman army from a militia conscripted for a particular campaign to a standing force of professional soldiers. Marius recruited from the unpropertied class and enlisted the proletarians, and yet this radical new army was borne of necessity, not design. The result was the accidental creation of the client army, although later generals (Sulla, Pompey, and Caesar) would use the loyalty of such soldiers to their personal advantage.

Marius' five successive consulships (in the years 104–100) challenged the Roman constitution to its very core and set a dangerous precedent. Sulla would eventually become dictator and conduct the bloodiest proscriptions Rome had ever endured. Perhaps in Marius and Sulla, Sallust saw the forebear of the young, energetic, charismatic Octavian who was, even as Sallust was writing, making his own history.

ꙮ *HISTORIAE*

After the monographs, Sallust finally turned to writing a more broadly conceived work covering events after the end of the war with Jugurtha and before the Catilinarian conspiracy. Unlike the *Bellum Iugurthinum* and the *Bellum Catilinae*, the *Historiae* does not survive as a complete text. Instead, only fragments have survived, either directly or indirectly. A codex from the second century CE in the Vatican library (*Codex Vaticanus Latinus* 3864) preserves a collection of speeches and letters from the works of Sallust; among these are six lengthy excerpts from the *Historiae*. The Fleury manuscript, written in Italy in the fifth century CE, originally held portions of the *Historiae* but was subsequently cut down in size for binding purposes; much of its contents were damaged. In 1979, the Vienna fragment from Book 1 (*Codex P. Vindobonae Latinus* 117) was published. Finally, two scraps of papyrus (*P. Rylands* III.473) contain one fragment of uncertain location and one from Book 2. Such is the direct transmission of the *Historiae* (see McGushin 1992, 5–7).

The bulk of the *Historiae* survives via indirect transmission, that is, by the quotations from and references to the text made by grammarians and commentators of late antiquity. As McGushin (1992, 7–10) explains, approximately 500 quotations derive from 46 sources, with the grammarians supplying over three-quarters of these. Nonius (early fourth century CE) provides 61 fragments of two lines or longer, many transmitted with book number. Servius (fourth century CE) provides 119 quotations in his magisterial commentary on the *Aeneid*; these quotations are usually only one line long, and only some are transmitted with book number. Arusianus Messius (late fourth century CE) preserves 106 fragments of only one line or less, all but three specify book number. Aelius Donatus (fourth century CE) preserves 32 fragments of one line or less, only six with book number. Finally, the early sixth century grammarian Priscian preserves 55 fragments of one line or less, only three without book number.

These grammarians quoted Sallust in order to illustrate a particular point of syntax, vocabulary, or diction rather than for historical content or import; as a result, the fragments that survive often demonstrate specific usages. It is not possible to determine norms or trends from such a highly selective sample. Therefore, the fragmentary state of the *Historiae* reminds us of a fundamental impediment to the study of antiquity. Not only has a great deal of Latin literature been lost, but every text depends on a precarious transmission through the ages.

The *Historiae*, as we have it, treats the years 78–67, that is, from the death of Sulla to the ratification of the *Lex Gabinia* that granted Pompey a three-year command and extraordinary resources to clear the seas of pirates. While the events of the *Bellum Catilinae* took place largely during the absence of Pompey from Rome, the *Historiae*, on the other hand, is essentially the story of his ascendancy (for Pompey's early career, see Seager 1979, 14–43).

Book 1 probably began with an introduction and a brief synopsis of events leading up to 78, followed by the revolt of the consul Marcus Aemilius Lepidus (father of the triumvir), who threatened to repeal the acts of Sulla. When Lepidus marched on Rome, the Senate appointed Pompey to lead an army against the rebel. Meanwhile, Quintus Sertorius, another anti-Sullan, set up an independent government in the province of Spain. Book 2 (77–74) included the final phase of Lepidus' revolt and a character sketch of Pompey, who was given command of the reinforcements sent to assist Caecilius Metellus Pius (son of Metellus Numidicus) against the rogue Sertorius. Book 3 covered the years 74–72, including the slave revolt led by the gladiator Spartacus. Although Marcus Licinius Crassus (praetor who later joined Pompey and Caesar in the so-called first triumvirate) was given command by the Senate and waged most of the war against Spartacus, Pompey, after merely rounding up the stragglers, took credit for the final victory. Book 4 (72–68) most likely continued the events of the third war against Mithridates VI. The extremely fragmentary Book 5 probably covered the years 68–67, including the pervasive pirate raids that ultimately interfered with Rome's grain supply. In hot debate, the Senate reluctantly passed the *Lex Gabinia*. Every episode of the extant *Historiae* seems to be designed to explain the development of the extraordinary career of Pompey.

The *Historiae* is a story of Rome's incompetence in the face of a series of political, social, and economic troubles. The revolt of Lepidus was a precursor to the Catilinarian conspiracy; Sertorius managed to control Spain and, with a counter-senate, to resist the post-Sullan regime for six years; Mithridates VI threatened Rome for decades before he finally committed suicide; a hapless band of pirates—stateless men—was able to disrupt the food supply; the slave rebellion of Spartacus, which began in 73 and was not crushed until 71, should never have been allowed to reach such proportions. In all of these conflicts, Pompey played a major role. But given the fragmentary nature of the *Historiae*, it is impossible to arrive at a conclusion about Sallust's treatment of this complex general.

∾ *Spurious works*

Two works attributed to Sallust are of dubious authenticity. The *Epistulae ad Caesarem senem de republica* are two letters of advice to Caesar. The *Inuectiuae in Ciceronem et in Sallustium* are orations in which Sallust and Cicero attack one another. As Syme demonstrates (1964, Appendix II), the letters cannot have been written by Sallust, because not only is their political terminology anachronistic, but their advice could not have been proffered by any prudent senator of the day. Rather, the works most likely derive from the schools of declamation of the early empire, in which teachers of rhetoric trained pupils for public speaking. The letters to Caesar are examples of *suasoriae*, a kind of exercise in which the student composed speeches advising a course of action in a historical, pseudo-historical, or mythological situation. The invectives are examples of *controversiae*, homework exercises in which the student composed speeches in character on both sides of a debate. Although the letters and orations are spurious, they attest to later generations' abiding interest in the life of Sallust and deep regard for his literary achievements (for further reading, see Walsh 1966).

∾ *Ancient historiography*

Although generally regarded as historical, the writings of Sallust differ from modern expectations of history; as a result, Sallust has been routinely condemned for his historical inaccuracy. Since the nineteenth century, empirical history has dominated, and modern historians strive for objective truth about the past based on data (the more quantitative, the better). Not so in antiquity: classical historiography is a literary genre, in which historians narrated past events as rhetorically as possible so as to persuade their readers of the importance of their ancestors and their contributions to the *res publica*. A less generous assessment would indict ancient historians of deliberate mendacity; however, the rules of the game were different, and judgment by modern standards is not fair. While it is possible to glean historical facts from ancient historiography, the precise reconstruction of political, social, or economic developments was not the primary aim. Rather, the ancient historians set out to provide examples of virtue, honor, and excellence to emulate or examples of vice, shame, and wickedness to avoid. Accordingly, ancient historiography is markedly moral in its tone.

∾ *Origin and development*

Sallust both conforms to, and deviates from, the expectations of the genre of ancient historiography that had developed over several centuries from Greece to Rome. According to Fornara (1983, 53–57), the Roman historians differ from their Greek counterparts in at least three ways. Roman historians had active political careers, making them informed sources. Second, they wrote about immediate events; whereas Greek history was broadly conceived across the known world, Roman history centered on the city foremost. Third, compared to the Greek historians, they had at their disposal a vast and accessible body of public records.

Traditionally, Quintus Fabius Pictor is credited as the first historian of Rome; he wrote in the second half of the third century. He is followed by Lucius Cincius Alimentus, Aulus Postumius Albinus, and Gaius Acilius. Although their writings survive only in mere scraps and fragments, it is worth recognizing these founders of the Roman historiographical tradition for one remarkable reason: they wrote in the Greek language! Presumably by writing Roman history in Greek, these historians promoted Roman culture and values to an increasingly Greek audience, as Roman conquest slowly progressed eastward across the Mediterranean. Marcus Porcius Cato (Cato the Censor, 234–149) pioneered the art of Latin prose and history writing in the Latin language.

The shift in language, from Greek to Latin, is accompanied by a shift in form as well, from annals to monograph. According to Cicero, "History began as a mere compilation of annals . . . the pontifex maximus used to commit to writing all the events of the year, record them on a white tablet, and post it up at his house so that the people might have liberty to become acquainted with it, and still today these records are called the *annales maximi*" (*De Oratore* 2.52). Over time, historians fleshed out these annalistic lists with episodes of cultural history, folktales, and *aetia*, or explanations for the origins of customs and institutions. The writing of history was also a way for an historian to recount and praise the achievements of his ancestors.

Lucius Coelius Antipater (late second century) appears to be the first Roman historian to reject the annalistic treatment of history in favor of the monograph that deals with a single topic. Lucius Cornelius Sisenna (118–67) wrote *Historiae* covering, as far as we can tell, the years 91–78. Thus, Coelius Antipater set a precedent for writing monographs, and Sisenna provided Sallust a starting point for his own *Historiae*. Therefore, although Sallust is the earliest Roman historian for whom complete works survive intact, it is imperative to remember that he is part of a well-established practice of history writing. His innovations are more readily recognized when we appreciate the tradition he inherited. (For a study of the fragmentary Roman historians from 240 to 63, see Becker 2008; for a brief introduction to Roman historiography and Sallust's place, see Kraus and Woodman 1997, 1–50).

∾ *Method*

In gathering information and composing his history, Sallust draws on a variety of material, both oral and written. Eyewitness (autopsy) and interview are the most prominent sources for contemporary events. Sallust can remember (*BC* 7.7) and testify first hand (*BC* 48.9). He can also consult men of the day (*BC* 22.1).

For older historical events, Sallust consults written sources (*BC* 9.4). He quotes letters which he seems to copy verbatim (*BC* 34.3, 44.4). Surely Sallust read the speeches of Cicero against Catiline, although he does not quote or even summarize their contents, presumably because of their popularity (*BC* 31.6). For information about the geography and peoples of Africa, Sallust consults books translated from Punic (*BI* 17.7). He declines to tell of the rise and domination of Sulla in detail, since Sisenna covered the period; however, he says he will correct Sisenna's biased narrative (*BI* 95.2). Indeed, in order to construct his own narrative authority, Sallust passes judgment on his predecessors. In the opening of his *Historiae*, Sallust attributes desirable qualities to other writers of history. Gaius Fannius was praised for his truth, Cato the Censor for his brevity, with whom Sallust aligns himself (*Hist.* 1.4; on Cato the Censor's influence on Sallust, see the excellent study of Levene 2000).

Sallust's method, therefore, consists of autopsy, interview, and documentary evidence; he consults previous scholarship for both facts and style. Above all, Sallust, like all ancient historians, engages in imaginative reconstruction or *inuentio* (contrivance). Rhetorical amplification was an acceptable way for ancient historians to develop the facts; the actual was further supported by the probable. "The invention of circumstantial detail," says Wiseman, "was a way to reach the truth" (1993, 146). Sallust does this two ways.

First, he shifts the point of view of the narrative, from his own authorial standpoint to the limited point of view of a particular character. The author (who knows, if not everything, at least more than the characters know at a given time) shifts to reveal only what a given character feels or knows. The historian does not have recourse to the inner thoughts of the character, but he can rely upon the probability of unspoken intentions as likely motivations for action. *Inuentio* allows Sallust to attribute causes and effects that, although they cannot be verified, are nonetheless believable. Nominative singular participles ("believing," "reckoning," "judging," "understanding," etc.) are particularly effective in achieving this almost imperceptible shift, and these are noted in the commentary.

Second, he skillfully, even artistically, constructs *topoi* (or set pieces). These are stock events that are a regular feature of the genre, for example, battles and their aftermath, sieges of cities, death, exile, geographical descriptions, sufferings and disasters, and perhaps most memorably, speeches. Sallust can amplify his account of a battle, for instance, by including the elements one normally expects: exhortation of troops, disposition of cavalry and infantry, attack, retreat, aftermath, and losses. In each component, the historian is at liberty to adorn the narrative so as to create verisimilitude, dignify the event, and engage and entertain the reader.

∿ *Content*

Prefaces are a regular feature of ancient historiography. The usual themes in prefaces include a praise of history, the reasons for choice of subject, and the historian's attitude to his work. In the preface, the reader learns why the author wrote history, how he regarded it, and what aims he intended to achieve. Sallust uses the preface to expound his moralizing philosophy. He begins his works with statements about human nature and the proper pursuits of life. For Sallust, the aristocratic ideal of *uirtus* is displayed in the activities of soldiers and statesmen alike, but after the fall of Carthage (in 146), Rome experienced a decline from the pristine state of *uirtus*. The expansion of the Roman empire brought the ambition, greed, and luxury that eroded the old morality. The recurrent theme in Sallust is the moral crisis of the late Republic, its causes and effects (see Earl 1961).

The preface to the *Bellum Catilinae* is proportionately the longest extant Latin prose preface; longer historical works begin with much less fanfare. The preface makes it clear that the outcome of the war with Catiline is as important as the moral issues that the conspiracy raises. The lengthy introduction justifies a work devoted to a subject that does not necessarily display all members of the Roman citizen body in the best possible light. Although in the end justice and good prevail, nevertheless the conspiracy demonstrates the grim potential for Roman society and morality to fall prey to violence and lawlessness. Sallust also takes care in the preface to situate himself in this moral landscape. He is careful to explain his own career and precarious fortunes so as to distance himself from the events he narrates—perhaps to the point of overcompensation (see Gunderson 2000).

Historical events are often the results of decisions made after heated debate, and so speeches are an integral part of ancient historiography. Statesmen debate policy, generals exhort the troops, demagogues incite the crowds. Although the ancient historians recount speeches, they were probably not present at the delivery, and even if they were, they cannot possibly provide a verbatim transcript. Thucydides said it best: "My method has been, while keeping as closely as possible to the general sense of the words that were actually used, to make the speakers say what, in my opinion, was called for by the situation" (1.22.1). Most historians, Sallust included, allude to this concession in abbreviated terms, trusting that their audience understands the convention. Therefore, as historians composed speeches, so history was a highly rhetorical genre.

Finally, ancient historiography regularly included descriptions of lands and peoples, and the excursus on the geography and people of North Africa (*BI* 17–19) is part of this literary tradition. From the fragments of the *Historiae*, we can piece together descriptions of Sardinia and Corsica (2.1–11), Taurus (2.82–86), Crete (3.10–15), Pontus (3.61–80), and the strait of Sicily known as "Scylla and Charybdis" (4.23–29). Geographical digressions were intended, in part, to entertain and delight the reader with tales of the curious, strange, and exotic. Yet the content of the descriptions has far less to tell us about the foreign peoples under examination than about the historians who produced them and the Romans who read them. Given the length of the African excursus and the five discernible geographical digressions in the fragments of the *Historiae*, the absence of geography in the *Bellum Catilinae* makes the internal conflict the more conspicuous. Conspiracy is one step away from civil war.

❧ *Sallust's language*

Sallust is famous for his archaism, the deliberate use of language that is old or obsolete. In this way he can scorn the nobility, so excessively proud of their ancestry, using the very language that their ancestors used. Archaism is evident in orthography:

quo- instead of *cu*- in words like *quom* (= *cum*), *quoius* (= *cuius*), or *quoi* (= *cui*)

-*os* instead of -*us* in the nom. sing. m.

-*om* instead of -*um* in the acc. sing.

-*u*- instead of -*i*- in superls. and other words, e.g., *optume, lubido*

-*undus* instead of -*endus* in gerunds and gerundives

-*o* instead of -*e*, for example, *uorto* (= *uerto*)

-*o* instead of -*u*, for example, *uoltus* (= *uultus*)

and morphology:

fore instead of *esse*, both as infinitive and in the imperfect subjunctive (see Lowrance 1931, 184–85)

uti, the older form of *ut*, the subordinate conjunction

the gen. sing. -*i* instead of -*ii* for most second-declension nouns in -*ius* or -*ium*

Some archaism is manifest in vocabulary as well; from this volume's selections, *prosapia* is the best example. Word order too lends an archaic flavor; for example, *igitur* is preferably post-positive (the second word in a sentence) in classical Latin, yet Sallust consistently imitates Cato the Censor and the earlier historians who regularly used *igitur* in initial position.

Diction conveys tone, and the political and social tenor of the times rings through Sallust's word choices. Some terms remind us vividly of the expanding Roman empire, for example, *terra marique* and its variant, *domi militiaeque*. The Mediterranean is referred to as *mare nostrum*. Simple words like *studium, stuprum*, or the combination *luxuria atque auaritia* convey complex notions and attitudes about Roman values and ethics. Such words can be translated easily enough with English equivalents ("eagerness," "sexual deviance," "luxury and greed"); however, it is worth bearing in mind the complex social implications that these words convey.

Sallust is at his best when deploying the relative clause of characteristic, a syntactical form distinct to the Latin language that describes a person of such a character that the statement is true of him or her and all others belonging to the same category. The relative clause with the subjunctive mood indicates a characteristic of the antecedent, especially when the antecedent is undefined. The relative clause of characteristic is also used after general expressions of existence;

for example, at *BC* 22.1, *fuere ea tempestate qui*, "there were those at the time who . . ." By expressing the characteristic in the subjunctive mood in a dependent clause, Sallust can avoid sounding bombastic or hyperbolic; instead, the relative clauses of characteristic tend to sound refined and judicious.

As an historian, Sallust's task is to explain causes, and so the selections abound with causal clauses in the indicative mood introduced by *quod.* Although *quod* is morphologically ambiguous (it is also the nom. or acc. sing. n. rel. pron.), its syntax is distinguished by the lack of antecedent, as well as by the presence of adverbs that anticipate a causal explanation.

In contrast to—or rather, because of—the simplicity of verb usage, Sallust's noun syntax is much more complex. In particular, the ablative case is used to its fullest potential. It provides a shorthand for comparison, so that with one word Sallust can express the object of comparison or the distance across which the difference is reckoned. So the ablative of degree of difference is Sallust's most elegant and critical mode of expression. English approximates the use, for example, "the more, the merrier." In this phrase, *the* is not the definite article but the instrumental case of the Anglo-Saxon pronoun *thæt*, "that." The pronoun is used both as relative (*by which, by how much*) and as demonstrative (*by that, by so much*). In fact, the English *the . . . the* corresponds exactly to the Latin ablative of degree of difference. The more students translate Sallust, the more comfortable they will become with this grammatical construction.

The number of adjectives occurring in the vocabulary is surprisingly low; of the more than 1,300 words in the vocabulary, only 161 are adjectives of the first and second declension, and only 60 third-declension adjectives are used. Thus, Sallust will use the ablative of description or genitive of quality instead of an adjective, and prepositional phrases or even adverbs will serve as predicate adjectives.

∾ *Sallust's style and influence*

No less than a command of grammar, a sensitivity to style contributes to reading comprehension, for by means of his style, Sallust conducts the individual parts of his grammatical orchestra to produce a symphony of majestic prose. Sallust's style is distinct for its *breuitas* (brevity) and *inconcinnitas* (unconnectedness).

Ancient rhetoricians coined the term *breuitas* to describe a particular style. *Breuitas* aids memory (shorter things are easier to remember), and so ancient authors used it to make their material more accessible to readers. The first rule of *breuitas* is to achieve only enough—*satis*: brevity is satisfying. Excess, whatever does not contribute to the reader's understanding of the matter, must be cut short. Thus, Sallust concludes his brief account of the so-called first Catilinarian conspiracy and his digression on Africa with the words *satis dictum*. Sallust also makes use of brief summary. Parataxis (coordinating clauses), apposition, and participles allow Sallust to move quickly through his material. *Breuitas* demands that the beginning of the work not indulge in background information but commence with a suitable stage of the event. Throughout the work, the author avoids repetition. The end of the work must take the reader only to the point where further narrative would no longer be relevant. *Breuitas* must never proceed at the expense of persuasion, and so a certain amount of ornament is necessary. Yet rhetorical flourishes must never be excessive; rather, they serve to make the long narrative appear short and to bolster probability. Finally, *breuitas* admits digressions—which must themselves observe the cardinal principles of *breuitas*—provided they are justified by the context. Indeed, the digressions in Sallust contain material that is integral not only to the narrative at hand but also to his philosophical conception of history.

Breuitas is exhibited at the most elemental levels. Sallust often omits *esse* (or *fore*) and *ut* (or *uti*) where context permits; he uses asyndeton far more than polysyndeton. With his plain vocabulary and relatively simple syntax, he is a master of simplicity. Periodic, or highly subordinated sentences, the hallmark of Cicero's grand oratorical style, are used sparingly (see Woodman 1988, 117–28, on Sallust's response to Ciceronian style).

Most striking, however, is the stark contrast between the perpetual antithesis that marks Sallust's thought and the *inconcinnitas* (lack of elegance or order) by which it is expressed. In the words of Syme, "Sallust is out to destroy balance and harmony" (1964, 265).

Grammatical parallelism is replaced by variation; for example, an adjective is paired with a prepositional phrase. The *uariatio* can be quite ornate, as at *BI* 19.1. In every instance, however, Sallust's variation is calculated for purpose and effect. Variation keeps the reader alert. By preferring tones that are slightly off-key, so to speak, Sallust can sound less practiced and so more sincere. Yet besides alertness and sincerity, *inconcinnitas* no doubt conveys disdain for the conventional. If Sallust seems to speak from moral high ground, it is in part because he holds common parlance at arm's length.

In spite of his brevity and unconnectedness, Sallust composes luxurious prose by means of his adroit use of standard figures of speech. The figures of speech that occur more than once in the selections include:

ALLITERATION: repetition of sound, especially consonants at the beginning of words; e.g., *flagitiis atque facinoribus* (*BC* 23.1)

ANAPHORA: repetition of words at the beginning of successive phrases or clauses; e.g., *pro pudore, pro abstinentia, pro uirtute* (*BC* 3.3)

ANASTROPHE: inversion of the usual order of words, such as prepositions following the object; e.g., *probri gratia* (*BC* 23.1).

ANNOMINATIO: etymologizing stem repetition; e.g., *simulator ac dissimulator* (*BC* 5.4)

ANTITHESIS: opposition, or contrast of parts; e.g., *satis eloquentia, sapientiae parum* (*BC* 5.4)

ASYNDETON: omission of coordinating conjunction; e.g., *a spe metu partibus* (*BC* 4.2).

BRACHYOLOGY: the absence of common elements, usually the finite verb, in one of two clauses; e.g., *quae illi litteris* (*BI* 85.13). Asyndeton and brachylogy are the chief means of achieving *breuitas*.

CHIASMUS: opposite word order (ABBA); e.g., *coniurationem aperit, nominat socios* (*BC* 40.6)

ENALLAGE: exchange or substitution of one grammatical form for another, in this volume's selections, the exchange of active and passive; e.g., *peteret . . . peteretur* (*BC* 25.3)

HYPERBATON: placement of a word outside of the clause in which it belongs; e.g., *Petreius ubi uidet Catilinam* (*BC* 60.5). Like anastrophe, hyperbaton helps create *inconcinnitas*.

LITOTES: affirmation by denial of the contrary; e.g., *haud obscuro loco* (*BC* 23.1)

PLEONASM: use of needless words; e.g., *tempore posterius* (*BI* 85.12). Sallust is rarely pleonastic, so that its use is all the more pointed.

TMESIS: separation of two parts of a compound word; e.g., *prius . . . quam* (*BC* 4.5). Tmesis gives Sallust more opportunity for *inconcinnitas*.

TRICOLON: a series of three phrases or clauses, the complexity of which can increase, decrease, or stay the same. Rarely are Sallust's tricola parallel or equal; instead, the tricolon affords an opportunity for *inconcinnitas*.

These definitions are not repeated in the commentary, and so students are advised to bookmark this list until they are able to identify figures of speech at sight. The beauty of Sallust's language lies not only in his adept deployment of these figures, but also in his ability to combine them to great effect; for example, antithesis emphasized by chiasmus.

Some of Sallust's style can be traced back to Greek literature. Readers both ancient and modern are consistently impressed by the abiding influence that the Greek historian Thucydides exerts on Sallust. The historian Velleius Paterculus, writing during the reign of the emperor Tiberius (14–37 CE), calls Sallust "the rival of Thucydides" (*History of Rome* 2.36.2). Quintilian is not afraid to compare Sallust to Thucydides (*Institutes of Oratory* 10.1.101). Scanlon's full-scale study of the influence of Thucydides on Sallust published in 1980 remains the authority. Both Thucydides and Sallust took up history writing for the same reason: they were generals forced out of politics into retirement. Both took up contemporary, selected events, rather than broadly sweeping, universal histories. Both deploy *breuitas* and *inconcinnitas*. For both historians, character explained causation, and character was best revealed through speeches. Beyond these formal similarities, however, Thucydides also shaped Sallust's philosophy of history. Like Thucydides, Sallust "discarded the supernatural" (Syme 1964, 246); human reason, passion, and emotion are more significant motivating factors than divinities or superstition. However, while Sallust may draw upon Thucydides for form, style, and outlook, in terms of storytelling and narrative technique, he more closely approximates Herodotus, as Grethlein has shown (2006a). Indeed, the traces of many Greek writers can be found in Sallust, including Aeschylus, Plato, and the Attic orators Lysias, Demosthenes, and Isocrates (Renehan 1976).

Sallust was widely read in antiquity. Vergil is fascinated by Catiline, whom he addresses directly at *Aeneid* 8.668; furthermore, as Ash (2002) suggests, the death of Helenor at *Aeneid* 9.544–55 recalls the death of Catiline. Writing during the reign of Tiberius, Valerius Maximus twice draws upon Sallust for anecdotes in his *Memorable Deeds and Sayings*. His example of Aulus Fulvius as a severe parent who visits harsh punishment upon his son derives no doubt from Sallust (5.8.5, cf. *BC* 39.5). Valerius also repeats the story that Catiline murdered his son so that he could marry Aurelia Orestilla (9.1.9, cf. *BC* 15.2). In his *Confessions* (2.5.11), Saint Augustine of Hippo compares his adolescent theft of the neighbor's pears to the madness of Catiline and quotes the *Bellum Catilinae*, proof that Sallust was an integral part of the grammar school curriculum.

Sallust's distinct style left an enduring impression upon subsequent historians. As Woodman (1969) has shown, he influenced the diction, tone, and theme of Velleius Paterculus. Tacitus adopted Sallust's terse asymmetry into the *Annals* so skillfully, especially in the character sketches and speeches, that it is sometimes difficult to tell where Sallustian imitation ends and Tacitean innovation begins. The late antique historian Orosius, brandishing Sallustian *breuitas*, cuts his account of the Catilinarian conspiracy short, "because Sallust's description is well known enough to everybody" (*Seven Books of History Against the Pagans,* 6.6.5–6). In the Renaissance, Sallust was an important historical and theoretical source for Machiavelli (Kapust 2007). For the nineteenth-century French dramatist and historian Prosper Mérimée, Sallust was the starting point for his study of the Catilinarian conspiracy: "I undertake, after Sallust, to narrate the Catilinarian conspiracy" (Lowrie 2008, 11).

Fig. 5. Statue of Gaius Sallustius Crispus. Piazza Palazzo, L'Aquila, Italy.

Beyond literature, however, Sallust left his mark. Whoever is fortunate enough to climb the Spanish Steps at Rome finds at the top an Egyptian obelisk, once located in the *horti Sallustiani* (Hartswick 2004, 52–53). The Austrian Parliament building in Vienna is adorned with statues of the ancient historians: Thucydides, Polybius, Xenophon, and Herodotus; Julius Caesar, Tacitus, Livy—and Sallust. Although the Italian city of L'Aquila was devastated by an earthquake on April 6, 2009, an ancient statue of Sallust still stands in front of the Palazzo Margherita in the Piazza Palazzo. The spirit of Sallust abides across both literature and landscape.

❧ *Suggested reading*

Allen, W. "Sallust's Political Career." *Studies in Philology* 51 (1954): 1–14.

———. "The Unity of the Sallustian Corpus." *Classical Journal* 61 (1966): 268–69.

Ash, R. "Epic Encounters? Ancient Historical Battle Narratives and the Epic Tradition." In *Clio and the Poets: Augustan Poetry and the Traditions of Ancient Historiography,* edited by D. Levene and D. Nelis, 253–73. Leiden, 2002.

Batstone, W. "*Quantum ingenio possum*: On Sallust's Use of *ingenium* in *Bellum Catilinae* 53.6." *Classical Journal* 83 (1988): 301–6.

———. "The Antithesis of Virtue: Sallust's *Synkrisis* and the Crisis of the Late Republic." *Classical Antiquity* 7 (1988a): 1–29.

Beard, M. *The Roman Triumph*. Cambridge, MA, 2007.

Becker, G. H. *Form, Intent, and the Fragmentary Roman Historians 240–63 BCE*. Ph.D. Dissertation, University of Florida, Gainesville, 2008.

Boyd, B. W. "*Virtus Effeminata* and Sallust's Sempronia." *Transactions of the American Philological Association* 117 (1987): 183–201.

Bradley, K. R. "Slaves and the Conspiracy of Catiline." *Classical Philology* 73 (1978): 329–36.

Braund, S. M. *Seneca: De Clementia*. Oxford, 2009.

Cadoux, T. "Sallust and Sempronia." In *Vindex Humanitatis: Essays in Honour of John Huntly Bishop*, edited by B. Marshall, 93–122. Armidale, 1980.

———. "Catiline and the Vestal Virgins." *Historia* 54 (2005): 162–79.

Claassen, J. M. "Sallust's Jugurtha: Rebel or Freedom Fighter? On Crossing Crocodile-Infested Waters." *Classical World* 86 (1993): 273–97.

Comber, M., and C. Balmaceda. *Sallust: The War Against Jugurtha*. Oxford, 2009.

Dué, C. "Tragic History and Barbarian Speech in Sallust's *Jugurtha*." *Harvard Studies in Classical Philology* 100 (2000): 311–25.

Earl, D. C. *The Political Thought of Sallust*. Cambridge, 1961.

Fields, B. M. "Sallust's *Bellum Iugurthinum*: Reading Jugurtha as the Other." M.A. Thesis, University of Florida, Gainesville, 2007.

Flower, H. I. *Ancestor Masks and Aristocratic Power in Roman Culture*. Oxford, 1996.

Fornara, C. W. *The Nature of History in Ancient Greece and Rome*. Berkeley, 1983.

Fowler, P. "Lucretian Conclusions." In *Classical Closure: Reading the End in Greek and Latin Literature*, edited by D. H. Roberts, F. M. Dunn, and D. Fower, 112–38. Princeton, 1997.

Frazer, R. M. "*Nam*-Clauses in Sallust." *Classical Philology* 56 (1961): 251–52.

Goodyear, F. R. D. "Sallust." In *The Cambridge History of Classical Literature,* Vol. 2: *Latin Literature*, edited by E. J. Kenney and W. V. Clausen, 268–80. Cambridge, 1982.

Green, C. M. C. "*De Africa et eius incolis:* The Function of Geography and Ethnography in Sallust's History of the Jugurthine War (*BJ* 17–19)." *Ancient World* 24 (1993): 185–97.

Grethlein, J. "*Nam quid ea memorem*: The Dialectical Relation of *res gestae* and *memoria rerum gestarum* in Sallust's *Bellum Jugurthinum*." *Classical Quarterly* 56 (2006): 135–48.

———. "The Unthucydidean Voice of Sallust." *TAPA* 136 (2006a): 299–327.

Gruen, E. S. *The Last Generation of the Roman Republic*. Berkeley, 1974.

Gunderson, E. "The History of Mind and the Philosophy of History in Sallust's *Bellum Catilinae*." *Ramus* 29 (2000): 85–126.

Habicht, C. *Cicero the Politician*. Baltimore, 1990.

Hardy, E. G. "The Catilinarian Conspiracy in Its Context: A Re-study of the Evidence." *Journal of Roman Studies* 7 (1917): 153–228.

Hartswick, K. J. *The Gardens of Sallust: A Changing Landscape*. Austin, 2004.

Hock, R. "Servile Behavior in Sallust's *Bellum Catilinae*." *Classical World* 82 (1988): 13–24.

Horsfall, N. "Illusion and Reality in Latin Topographical Writing." *Greece & Rome* 32 (1985): 197–208.

Kapust, D. "Cato's Virtues and *The Prince*: Reading Sallust's *War with Catiline* with Machiavelli's *The Prince*." *History of Political Thought* 28 (2007): 433–48.

Katz, B. R. "Did Sallust Have a Guilty Conscience?" *Eranos* 81 (1983): 101–11.

Konstan, D. "Clemency as a Virtue." *Classical Philology* 100 (2005): 337–46.

Kraus, C. S. "Jugurthine Disorder." In *The Limits of Historiography*, edited by C. S. Kraus, 217–47. Leiden, 1999.

Kraus, C. S. and A. J. Woodman. *Latin Historians*. Oxford, 1997.

Last, H. M. "Sallust and Caesar in the *Bellum Catilinae*." In *Mélanges de philologie, de littérature et d'histoire anciennes offerts à J. Marouzeau*, 355–69. Paris, 1948.

Leigh, M. "Wounding and Popular Rhetoric at Rome." *Bulletin of the Institute of Classical Studies* 40 (1995): 195–212.

Levene, D. S. "Sallust's *Jugurtha*: An 'Historical Fragment.'" *Journal of Roman Studies* 82 (1992): 53–70.

———. "Sallust's *Catiline* and Cato the Censor." *Classical Quarterly* 50 (2000): 170–91.

Lowrance, W. D. "The Use of *Forem* and *Essem*." *Transactions and Proceedings of the American Philological Association* 62 (1931): 169–91.

Lowrie, M. "Evidence and Narrative in Mérimée's *Catilinarian Conspiracy*." *New German Critique* 103 (2008): 9–25.

Marincola, J. *Authority and Tradition in Ancient Historiography*. Cambridge, 1997.

———. "Genre, Convention, and Innovation in Greco-Roman Historiography." In *The Limits of Historiography*, edited by C. S. Kraus, 281–324. Leiden, 1999.

Marshall, B. A. "The Date of Catiline's Marriage to Aurelia Orestilla." *Rivista di Filologia e di Istruzione Classica* 105 (1977): 151–54.

Matthews, V. J. "The *Libri Punici* of King Hiempsal." *American Journal of Philology* 93 (1972): 330–35.

McGushin, P. *Sallust: The Histories, Volume 1: Books i–ii*, translated with introduction and commentary. Oxford, 1992.

Miller, N. P. "Dramatic Speech in the Roman Historians." *Greece & Rome* 22 (1975): 45–57.

Morstein-Marx, R. "The Alleged 'Massacre' at Cirta and Its Consequences (Sallust *Bellum Iugurthinum* 26–27)." *Classical Philology* 95 (2000): 468–76.

———. "The Myth of Numidian Origins in Sallust's African Excursus (*Iugurtha* 17.7–18.12)." *American Journal of Philology* 122 (2001): 179–200.

———. *Mass Oratory and Political Power in the Late Roman Republic.* Cambridge, 2004.

Osgood, J. *Caesar's Legacy: Civil War and the Emergence of the Roman Empire.* Cambridge, 2006.

Pagán, V. E. "The Mourning After: Statius *Thebaid* 12." *American Journal of Philology* 121 (2000): 423–52.

———. *Conspiracy Narratives in Roman History.* Austin, 2004.

Paul, G. M. "Sallust's Sempronia: The Portrait of a Lady." *Papers of the Liverpool Latin Seminar* 5 (1985): 9–22.

Phang, S. E. *Roman Military Service: Ideologies of Discipline in the Late Republic and Early Principate.* Cambridge, 2008.

Ramsey, J. T. *Sallust's Bellum Catilinae*, 2nd edition. Oxford, 2007.

Renehan, R. "A Traditional Pattern of Imitation in Sallust and His Sources." *Classical Philology* 71 (1976): 97–105.

Santoro-L'hoir, F. *The Rhetoric of Gender Terms: "Man," "Woman," and the Portrayal of Character in Latin Prose.* Leiden, 1992.

Scanlon, T. F. *The Influence of Thucydides on Sallust.* Heidelberg, 1980.

Seager, R. "The First Catilinarian Conspiracy." *Historia* 13 (1964): 338–47.

———. *Pompey: A Political Biography.* Berkeley, 1979.

Shaw, B. D. "Debt in Sallust." *Latomus* 34 (1975): 187–96.

Skard, E. "Marius' Speech in Sallust, Jug. chap. 85." *Symbolae Osloenses* 21 (1941): 98–102.

Sklenář, R. "*La République des Signes:* Caesar, Cato, and the Language of Sallustian Morality." *Transactions of the American Philological Association* 128 (1998): 205–20.

Syme, R. *The Roman Revolution.* Oxford, 1939.

———. *Sallust.* Berkeley, 1964.

Tan, J. "*Contiones* in the Age of Cicero." *Classical Antiquity* 27 (2008): 163–201.

Taylor, L. R. *Roman Voting Assemblies from the Hannibalic War to the Dictatorship of Caesar.* Ann Arbor, 1966.

Thomas, R. F. *Lands and Peoples in Roman Poetry: The Ethnographical Tradition.* Cambridge, 1982.

Treggiari, S. *Roman Marriage: Iusti Coniuges from the Time of Cicero to the Time of Ulpian.* Oxford, 1991.

Vasaly, A. *Representations: Images of the World in Ciceronian Oratory.* Berkeley, 1993.

von Fritz, K. "Sallust and the Attitude of the Roman Nobility at the Time of the Wars against Jugurtha (112–105 B.C.)." *Transactions and Proceedings of the American Philological Association* 74 (1943): 134–68.

Walsh, P. G. "Sallust." In *Latin Historians*, edited by T. A. Dorey, 85–113. London, 1966.

Waters, K. H. "Cicero, Sallust and Catiline." *Historia* 19 (1970): 195–215 (not cited, but worth consulting for its revisionist argument: there *was* no such thing as a Catilinarian conspiracy)

Wiedemann, T. "Sallust's *Jugurtha*: Concord, Discord, and the Digressions." *Greece & Rome* 40 (1993): 48–57.

Wilkins, A. T. *Villain or Hero: Sallust's Portrayal of Catiline.* New York, 1994.

Williams, K. F. "Manlius' *Mandata*: Sallust *Bellum Catilinae* 33." *Classical Philology* 95 (2000) 160–71.

Wiseman, T. P. "Lying Historians: Seven Types of Mendacity." In *Lies and Fiction in the Ancient World*, edited by C. Gill and T. P. Wiseman, 122–46. Austin, 1993.

Woodman, A. J. "Sallustian Influence on Velleius Paterculus." In *Hommages à Marcel Renard*, edited by J. Bibauw, vol. 1 (1969): 785–99.

———. *Rhetoric in Classical Historiography: Four Studies.* Portland, OR, 1988.

———. *Sallust: Catiline's War, The Jugurthine War, Histories*, translated with an introduction and notes. London, 2007.

Yavetz, Z. "The Failure of Catiline's Conspiracy." *Historia* 12 (1963): 485–99.

Latin Text

The text is from L. D. Reynolds, *C. Sallusti Crispi Catilina, Iugurtha, Historiarum Fragmenta Selecta, Appendix Sallustiana*. Oxford, 1991. I have retained his spelling throughout. I diverge from his text in three places in the selections:

> *BC* 29.1 **exagitatum** for **exagitatam**
>
> *BC* 53.5 **sua** for **sui**
>
> *BI* 85.47 **in** for **[in]**

∾ *Bellum Catilinae*

3.3–4.5

1   Sed ego adulescentulus initio, sicuti plerique, studio ad   **3.3**
rem publicam latus sum, ibique mihi multa aduorsa fuere.
Nam pro pudore, pro abstinentia, pro uirtute audacia
largitio auaritia uigebant. Quae tametsi animus asperna-   **4**
5 batur insolens malarum artium, tamen inter tanta uitia
inbecilla aetas ambitione corrupta tenebatur; ac me, quom   **5**
ab relicuorum malis moribus dissentirem, nihilo minus
honoris cupido eadem qua ceteros fama atque inuidia
uexabat. Igitur ubi animus ex multis miseriis atque   **4.1**
10 periculis requieuit et mihi relicuam aetatem a re publica
procul habendam decreui, non fuit consilium socordia
atque desidia bonum otium conterere, neque uero agrum
colundo aut uenando, seruilibus officiis, intentum aetatem
agere; sed a quo incepto studioque me ambitio mala   **2**

15 detinuerat, eodem regressus statui res gestas populi

Romani carptim, ut quaeque memoria digna uidebantur,

perscribere, eo magis quod mihi a spe metu partibus rei

publicae animus liber erat.

    Igitur de Catilinae coniuratione quam uerissume potero   3

20 paucis absoluam; nam id facinus in primis ego memora-   4

bile existumo sceleris atque periculi nouitate. De quoius   5

hominis moribus pauca prius explananda sunt quam

initium narrandi faciam.

5.1–8

1   L. Catilina, nobili genere natus, fuit magna ui et animi   5.1

et corporis, sed ingenio malo prauoque. Huic ab adu-   2

lescentia bella intestina caedes rapinae discordia ciuilis

grata fuere, ibique iuuentutem suam exercuit. Corpus   3

5 patiens inediae algoris uigiliae supra quam quoiquam

credibile est. Animus audax subdolus uarius, quoius rei   4

lubet simulator ac dissimulator, alieni adpetens sui

profusus, ardens in cupiditatibus; satis eloquentiae,

sapientiae parum. Vastus animus inmoderata incredibilia   5

10 nimis alta semper cupiebat. Hunc post dominationem L.   6

Sullae lubido maxuma inuaserat rei publicae capiundae,

neque id quibus modis adsequeretur, dum sibi regnum

pararet, quicquam pensi habebat. Agitabatur magis   7

magisque in dies animus ferox inopia rei familiaris et

15 conscientia scelerum, quae utraque iis artibus auxerat

quas supra memoraui. Incitabant praeterea corrupti ciui-   8

tatis mores, quos pessuma ac diuorsa inter se mala, luxuria

atque auaritia, uexabant.

15

1   Iam primum adulescens Catilina multa nefanda stupra   **15.1**
fecerat, cum uirgine nobili, cum sacerdote Vestae, alia
huiusce modi contra ius fasque. Postremo captus amore   2
Aureliae Orestillae, quoius praeter formam nihil umquam
5 bonus laudauit, quod ea nubere illi dubitabat timens
priuignum adulta aetate, pro certo creditur necato filio
uacuam domum scelestis nuptiis fecisse. Quae quidem res   3
mihi in primis uidetur causa fuisse facinus maturandi;
namque animus inpurus, dis hominibusque infestus,   4
10 neque uigiliis neque quietibus sedari poterat: ita conscientia mentem excitam uastabat. Igitur colos exsanguis, foedi   5
oculi, citus modo, modo tardus incessus: prorsus in facie
uoltuque uecordia inerat.

22

1   Fuere ea tempestate qui dicerent Catilinam, oratione   **22.1**
habita, quom ad ius iurandum popularis sceleris sui
adigeret, humani corporis sanguinem uino permixtum in
pateris circumtulisse, inde quom post execrationem   2
5 omnes degustauissent, sicuti in sollemnibus sacris fieri
consueuit, aperuisse consilium suom [atque eo dictitare
fecisse] quo inter se fidi magis forent, alius alii tanti
facinoris conscii. Nonnulli ficta et haec et multa praeterea   3
existumabant ab iis qui Ciceronis inuidiam, quae postea
10 orta est, leniri credebant atrocitate sceleris eorum qui
poenas dederant. Nobis ea res pro magnitudine parum
conperta est.

23–24

1   Sed in ea coniuratione fuit Q. Curius, natus haud   **23.1**

obscuro loco, flagitiis atque facinoribus coopertus, quem

censores senatu probri gratia mouerant. Huic homini non   **2**

minor uanitas inerat quam audacia: neque reticere quae

5   audierat neque suamet ipse scelera occultare, prorsus

neque dicere neque facere quicquam pensi habebat. Erat   **3**

ei cum Fuluia, muliere nobili, stupri uetus consuetudo;

quoi cum minus gratus esset quia inopia minus largiri

poterat, repente glorians maria montisque polliceri coepit

10   et minari interdum ferro, ni sibi obnoxia foret, postremo

ferocius agitare quam solitus erat. At Fuluia insolentiae   **4**

Curi causa cognita tale periculum rei publicae haud

occultum habuit, sed sublato auctore de Catilinae coniu-

ratione quae quoque modo audierat compluribus narrauit.

15   Ea res in primis studia hominum adcendit ad consu-   **5**

latum mandandum M. Tullio Ciceroni. Namque antea   **6**

pleraque nobilitas inuidia aestuabat, et quasi pollui con-

sulatum credebant, si eum quamuis egregius homo nouos

adeptus foret; sed ubi periculum aduenit, inuidia atque

20   superbia post fuere.

Igitur comitiis habitis consules declarantur M. Tullius   **24.1**

et C. Antonius; quod factum primo popularis coniuratio-

nis concusserat. Neque tamen Catilinae furor minuebatur,   **2**

sed in dies plura agitare, arma per Italiam locis opportunis

25   parare, pecuniam sua aut amicorum fide sumptam

mutuam Faesulas ad Manlium quendam portare, qui

postea princeps fuit belli faciundi. Ea tempestate pluru-   **3**

mos quoiusque generis homines adsciuisse sibi dicitur,
mulieres etiam aliquot, quae primo ingentis sumptus
30 stupro corporis tolerauerant, post, ubi aetas tantummodo
quaestui neque luxuriae modum fecerat, aes alienum
grande conflauerant. Per eas se Catilina credebat posse   4
seruitia urbana sollicitare, urbem incendere, uiros earum
uel adiungere sibi uel interficere. ⌐

25

1 Sed in iis erat Sempronia, quae multa saepe uirilis   **25.1**
audaciae facinora conmiserat. Haec mulier genere atque   2
forma, praeterea uiro liberis satis fortunata fuit; litteris
Graecis [et] Latinis docta, psallere [et] saltare elegantius
5 quam necesse est probae, multa alia quae instrumenta
luxuriae sunt. Sed ei cariora semper omnia quam decus   3
atque pudicitia fuit; pecuniae an famae minus parceret
haud facile discerneres; lubido sic adcensa ut saepius
peteret uiros quam peteretur. Sed ea saepe antehac fidem   4
10 prodiderat, creditum abiurauerat, caedis conscia fuerat:
luxuria atque inopia praeceps abierat. Verum ingenium   5
eius haud absurdum: posse uersus facere, iocum mouere,
sermone uti uel modesto uel molli uel procaci; prorsus
multae facetiae multusque lepos inerat.

27.2–29

1 Interea Romae multa simul moliri: consulibus insidias   **27.2**
tendere, parare incendia, opportuna loca armatis homini-
bus obsidere; ipse cum telo esse, item alios iubere, hortari

uti semper intenti paratique essent; dies noctisque festi-

5   nare uigilare, neque insomniis neque labore fatigari. Post-   3
remo, ubi multa agitanti nihil procedit, rursus intempesta
nocte coniurationis principes conuocat per M. Porcium
Laecam, ibique multa de ignauia eorum questus docet se   4
Manlium praemisisse ad eam multitudinem quam ad
10   capiunda arma parauerat, item alios in alia loca opportuna
qui initium belli facerent, seque ad exercitum proficisci
cupere, si prius Ciceronem oppressisset: eum suis con-
siliis multum officere. Igitur perterritis ac dubitantibus   28.1
ceteris C. Cornelius eques Romanus operam suam polli-
15   citus et cum eo L. Vargunteius senator constituere ea
nocte paulo post cum armatis hominibus sicuti salutatum
introire ad Ciceronem ac de inprouiso domi suae inparatum confodere. Curius ubi intellegit quantum periculum   2
consuli inpendeat, propere per Fuluiam Ciceroni dolum
20   qui parabatur enuntiat. Ita illi ianua prohibiti tantum   3
facinus frustra susceperant.

Interea Manlius in Etruria plebem sollicitare, egestate   4
simul ac dolore iniuriae nouarum rerum cupidam, quod
Sullae dominatione agros bonaque omnia amiserat, prae-
25   terea latrones quoiusque generis, quorum in ea regione
magna copia erat, nonnullos ex Sullanis coloniis quibus
lubido atque luxuria ex magnis rapinis nihil relicui fecerat.

Ea cum Ciceroni nuntiarentur, ancipiti malo permotus,   29.1
quod neque urbem ab insidiis priuato consilio longius
30   tueri poterat neque exercitus Manli quantus aut quo consilio foret satis conpertum habebat, rem ad senatum refert,

iam antea uolgi rumoribus exagitatum. Itaque, quod　　2
plerumque in atroci negotio solet, senatus decreuit, darent
operam consules ne quid res publica detrimenti caperet.

35　Ea potestas per senatum more Romano magistratui　　3
maxuma permittitur: exercitum parare, bellum gerere,
coercere omnibus modis socios atque ciuis, domi militiaeque imperium atque iudicium summum habere; aliter
sine populi iussu nullius earum rerum consuli ius est.

40–41

1　　　　　　　　　Igitur P. Vmbreno quoidam　　40.1
negotium dat uti legatos Allobrogum requirat eosque, si
possit, inpellat ad societatem belli, existumans publice
priuatimque aere alieno oppressos, praeterea quod natura
5　gens Gallica bellicosa esset, facile eos ad tale consilium
adduci posse. Vmbrenus, quod in Gallia negotiatus erat,　　2
plerisque principibus ciuitatium notus erat atque eos
nouerat. Itaque sine mora, ubi primum legatos in foro con-
spexit, percontatus pauca de statu ciuitatis et quasi dolens
10　eius casum requirere coepit quem exitum tantis malis
sperarent. Postquam illos uidet queri de auaritia magis-　　3
tratuum, accusare senatum quod in eo auxili nihil esset,
miseriis suis remedium mortem expectare, 'At ego' inquit
'uobis, si modo uiri esse uoltis, rationem ostendam qua
15　tanta ista mala effugiatis'. Haec ubi dixit, Allobroges in　　4
maxumam spem adducti Vmbrenum orare ut sui misereretur: nihil tam asperum neque tam difficile esse quod non
cupidissume facturi essent, dum ea res ciuitatem aere

alieno liberaret. Ille eos in domum D. Bruti perducit, quod   5

20 foro propinqua erat neque aliena consili propter Sem-

proniam; nam tum Brutus <ab> Roma aberat. Praeterea   6

Gabinium arcessit, quo maior auctoritas sermoni inesset.

Eo praesente coniurationem aperit, nominat socios,

praeterea multos quoiusque generis innoxios, quo legatis

25 animus amplior esset. Deinde eos pollicitos operam suam

domum dimittit. Sed Allobroges diu in incerto habuere   41.1

quidnam consili caperent. In altera parte erat aes alienum,   2

studium belli, magna merces in spe uictoriae; at in altera

maiores opes, tuta consilia, pro incerta spe certa praemia.

30 Haec illis uoluentibus tandem uicit fortuna rei publicae.   3

Itaque Q. Fabio Sangae, quoius patrocinio ciuitas pluru-   4

mum utebatur, rem omnem uti cognouerant aperiunt.

Cicero per Sangam consilio cognito legatis praecepit ut   5

studium coniurationis uehementer simulent, ceteros

35 adeant, bene polliceantur dentque operam uti eos quam

maxume manufestos habeant.

53–54

1   Postquam Cato adsedit, consulares omnes itemque   53.1

senatus magna pars sententiam eius laudant, uirtutem

animi ad caelum ferunt, alii alios increpantes timidos

uocant. Cato clarus atque magnus habetur; senati decre-

5 tum fit sicuti ille censuerat.

Sed mihi multa legenti, multa audienti quae populus   2

Romanus domi militiaeque, mari atque terra praeclara

facinora fecit, forte lubuit adtendere quae res maxume

tanta negotia sustinuisset. Sciebam saepenumero parua   3

10 manu cum magnis legionibus hostium contendisse; cog-
noueram paruis copiis bella gesta cum opulentis regibus,
ad hoc saepe fortunae uiolentiam tolerauisse, facundia
Graecos, gloria belli Gallos ante Romanos fuisse. Ac mihi   4
multa agitanti constabat paucorum ciuium egregiam

15 uirtutem cuncta patrauisse, eoque factum uti diuitias
paupertas, multitudinem paucitas superaret. Sed post-   5
quam luxu atque desidia ciuitas corrupta est, rursus res
publica magnitudine sua imperatorum atque magistratuum uitia sustentabat ac, sicuti †effeta parentum†, multis

20 tempestatibus haud sane quisquam Romae uirtute magnus
fuit. Sed memoria mea ingenti uirtute, diuorsis moribus   6
fuere uiri duo, M. Cato et C. Caesar. Quos quoniam res
obtulerat, silentio praeterire non fuit consilium, quin
utriusque naturam et mores, quantum ingenio possum,

25 aperirem.

Igitur iis genus aetas eloquentia prope aequalia fuere,   **54.1**
magnitudo animi par, item gloria, sed alia alii. Caesar   2
beneficiis ac munificentia magnus habebatur, integritate
uitae Cato. Ille mansuetudine et misericordia clarus

30 factus, huic seueritas dignitatem addiderat. Caesar dando   3
subleuando ignoscundo, Cato nihil largiundo gloriam
adeptus est. In altero miseris perfugium erat, in altero
malis pernicies. Illius facilitas, huius constantia lauda-
batur. Postremo Caesar in animum induxerat laborare,   4

35 uigilare; negotiis amicorum intentus sua neglegere, nihil
denegare quod dono dignum esset; sibi magnum im-

perium, exercitum, bellum nouom exoptabat ubi uirtus

enitescere posset. At Catoni studium modestiae, decoris,   5

sed maxume seueritatis erat; non diuitiis cum diuite neque   6

40 factione cum factioso, sed cum strenuo uirtute, cum

modesto pudore, cum innocente abstinentia certabat; esse

quam uideri bonus malebat: ita, quo minus petebat

gloriam, eo magis illum sequebatur.

60–61

1   Sed ubi omnibus rebus exploratis Petreius tuba signum   60.1

dat, cohortis paulatim incedere iubet; idem facit hostium

exercitus. Postquam eo uentum est unde a ferentariis   2

proelium conmitti posset, maxumo clamore cum infestis

5   signis concurrunt; pila omittunt, gladiis res geritur.

Veterani pristinae uirtutis memores comminus acriter   3

instare; illi haud timidi resistunt; maxuma ui certatur.

Interea Catilina cum expeditis in prima acie uorsari,   4

laborantibus succurrere, integros pro sauciis arcessere,

10 omnia prouidere, multum ipse pugnare, saepe hostem

ferire: strenui militis et boni imperatoris officia simul

exequebatur. Petreius ubi uidet Catilinam, contra ac ratus   5

erat, magna ui tendere, cohortem praetoriam in medios

hostis inducit eosque perturbatos atque alios alibi

15 resistentis interficit; deinde utrimque ex lateribus ceteros

adgreditur. Manlius et Faesulanus in primis pugnantes   6

cadunt. <Catilina>, postquam fusas copias seque cum   7

paucis relicuom uidet, memor generis atque pristinae suae

dignitatis, in confertissumos hostis incurrit ibique pugnans

20 confoditur.

Sed confecto proelio, tum uero cerneres quanta audacia   **61.1**

quantaque animi uis fuisset in exercitu Catilinae. Nam   2

fere quem quisque uiuos pugnando locum ceperat, eum

amissa anima corpore tegebat. Pauci autem, quos medios   3

25 cohors praetoria disiecerat, paulo diuorsius, sed omnes

tamen aduorsis uolneribus conciderant. Catilina uero   4

longe a suis inter hostium cadauera repertus est, paululum

etiam spirans ferociamque animi quam habuerat uiuos in

uoltu retinens. Postremo ex omni copia neque in proelio   5

30 neque in fuga quisquam ciuis ingenuos captus est: ita   6

cuncti suae hostiumque uitae iuxta pepercerant. Neque   7

tamen exercitus populi Romani laetam aut incruentam

uictoriam adeptus erat; nam strenuissumus quisque aut

occiderat in proelio aut grauiter uolneratus discesserat.

35 Multi autem, qui e castris uisundi aut spoliandi gratia   8

processerant, uoluentes hostilia cadauera, amicum alii,

pars hospitem aut cognatum reperiebant; fuere item qui

inimicos suos cognoscerent. Ita uarie per omnem exerci-   9

tum laetitia, maeror, luctus atque gaudia agitabantur.

❧ *Bellum Iugurthinum*

6–7

1   Qui ubi primum adoleuit, pollens uiribus, decora facie,   **6.1**

sed multo maxume ingenio ualidus, non se luxu neque

inertiae corrumpendum dedit, sed, uti mos gentis illius

est, equitare, iaculari, cursu cum aequalibus certare, et

5   quom omnis gloria anteiret, omnibus tamen carus esse; ad

hoc pleraque tempora in uenando agere, leonem atque

alias feras primus aut in primis ferire, plurumum facere,

[et] minumum ipse de se loqui. Quibus rebus Micipsa   **2**

tametsi initio laetus fuerat, existumans uirtutem Iugurthae

10   regno suo gloriae fore, tamen, postquam hominem adules-

centem exacta sua aetate et paruis liberis magis magisque

crescere intellegit, uehementer eo negotio permotus multa

cum animo suo uoluebat. Terrebat eum natura mortalium   **3**

auida imperi et praeceps ad explendam animi cupidinem,

15   praeterea opportunitas suae liberorumque aetatis, quae

etiam mediocris uiros spe praedae transuorsos agit, ad hoc

studia Numidarum in Iugurtham adcensa, ex quibus, si

talem uirum dolis interfecisset, ne qua seditio aut bellum

oriretur anxius erat.

20   His difficultatibus circumuentus, ubi uidet neque per   **7.1**

uim neque insidiis opprimi posse hominem tam acceptum

popularibus, quod erat Iugurtha manu promptus et ad-

petens gloriae militaris, statuit eum obiectare periculis et

eo modo fortunam temptare. Igitur bello Numantino   **2**

25   Micipsa, quom populo Romano equitum atque peditum

auxilia mitteret, sperans uel ostentando uirtutem uel

hostium saeuitia facile eum occasurum, praefecit Numidis

quos in Hispaniam mittebat. Sed ea res longe aliter ac   **3**

ratus erat euenit. Nam Iugurtha, ut erat inpigro atque acri   **4**

30 ingenio, ubi naturam P. Scipionis, qui tum Romanis

imperator erat, et morem hostium cognouit, multo labore

multaque cura, praeterea modestissume parendo et saepe

obuiam eundo periculis in tantam claritudinem breui

peruenerat ut nostris uehementer carus, Numantinis

35 maxumo terrori esset. Ac sane, quod difficillumum in   **5**

primis est, et proelio strenuos erat et bonus consilio,

quorum alterum ex prouidentia timorem, alterum ex

audacia temeritatem adferre plerumque solet. Igitur   **6**

imperator omnis fere res asperas per Iugurtham agere, in

40 amicis habere, magis magisque eum in dies amplecti,

quippe quoius neque consilium neque inceptum ullum

frustra erat. Huc adcedebat munificentia animi et ingeni   **7**

sollertia, quis rebus sibi multos ex Romanis familiari

amicitia coniunxerat.

17–19

1 Res postulare uidetur Africae situm paucis exponere et   **17.1**

eas gentis quibuscum nobis bellum aut amicitia fuit adtin-

gere. Sed quae loca et nationes ob calorem aut asperi-   **2**

tatem, item solitudines minus frequentata sunt, de iis haud

5 facile conpertum narrauerim; cetera quam paucissumis

absoluam.

In diuisione orbis terrae plerique in parte tertia Africam   **3**

posuere, pauci tantummodo Asiam et Europam esse, sed

Africam in Europa. Ea finis habet ab occidente fretum   4

10 nostri maris et Oceani, ab ortu solis decliuem latitudinem,

quem locum Catabathmon incolae appellant. Mare   5

saeuom, inportuosum; ager frugum fertilis, bonus pecori,

arbori infecundus; caelo terraque penuria aquarum.

Genus hominum salubri corpore, uelox, patiens laborum;   6

15 plerosque senectus dissoluit, nisi qui ferro aut bestiis

interiere, nam morbus haud saepe quemquam superat. Ad

hoc malefici generis pluruma animalia.

Sed qui mortales initio Africam habuerint quique   7

postea adcesserint aut quo modo inter se permixti sint,

20 quamquam ab ea fama quae plerosque obtinet diuorsum

est, tamen uti ex libris Punicis qui regis Hiempsalis dice-

bantur interpretatum nobis est, utique rem sese habere

cultores eius terrae putant, quam paucissumis dicam.

Ceterum fides eius rei penes auctores erit.

25 Africam initio habuere Gaetuli et Libyes, asperi incul-   **18.1**

tique, quis cibus erat caro ferina atque humi pabulum uti

pecoribus. Ii neque moribus neque lege aut imperio   2

quoiusquam regebantur; uagi, palantes, quas nox coege-

rat sedes habebant. Sed postquam in Hispania Hercules,   3

30 sicuti Afri putant, interiit, exercitus eius, conpositus ex

uariis gentibus, amisso duce ac passim multis sibi

quisque imperium petentibus, breui dilabitur. Ex eo   4

numero Medi, Persae et Armenii nauibus in Africam

transuecti proxumos nostro mari locos occupauere, sed   5

35 Persae intra Oceanum magis, iique alueos nauium in-

uorsos pro tuguriis habuere, quia neque materia in agris

neque ab Hispanis emundi aut mutandi copia erat: mare   **6**

magnum et ignara lingua conmercio prohibebant. Ii   **7**

paulatim per conubia Gaetulos secum miscuere et, quia

40 saepe temptantes agros alia, deinde alia loca petiuerant,

semet ipsi Nomadas appellauere. Ceterum adhuc aedificia   **8**

Numidarum agrestium, quae mapalia illi uocant, oblonga,

incuruis lateribus tecta, quasi nauium carinae sunt. Medis   **9**

autem et Armeniis adcessere Libyes—nam ii propius mare

45 Africum agitabant, Gaetuli sub sole magis, haud procul ab

ardoribus—iique mature oppida habuere; nam freto diuisi

ab Hispania mutare res inter se instituerant. Nomen   **10**

eorum paulatim Libyes corrupere, barbara lingua Mauros

pro Medis appellantes. Sed res Persarum breui adoleuit,   **11**

50 ac postea nomine Numidae, propter multitudinem a

parentibus digressi, possedere ea loca, quae proxuma

Carthaginem Numidia appellatur. Deinde utrique alteris   **12**

freti finitumos armis aut metu sub imperium suom

coegere, nomen gloriamque sibi addidere, magis ii qui ad

55 nostrum mare processerant, quia Libyes quam Gaetuli

minus bellicosi. Denique Africae pars inferior pleraque ab

Numidis possessa est, uicti omnes in gentem nomenque

imperantium concessere.

    Postea Phoenices, alii multitudinis domi minuendae   **19.1**

60 gratia, pars imperi cupidine, sollicitata plebe et aliis

nouarum rerum auidis, Hipponem Hadrumetum Leptim

aliasque urbis in ora marituma condidere, eaeque breui

multum auctae, pars originibus suis praesidio, aliae decori

fuere. Nam de Carthagine silere melius puto quam parum   **2**

65 dicere, quoniam alio properare tempus monet.

Igitur ad Catabathmon, qui locus Aegyptum ab Africa   3
diuidit, secundo mari prima Cyrene est, colonia Theraeon, ac deinceps duae Syrtes interque eas Leptis, deinde
Philaenon arae, quem locum Aegyptum uorsus finem
70 imperi habuere Carthaginienses, post aliae Punicae urbes.
Cetera loca usque ad Mauretaniam Numidae tenent,   4
proxumi Hispanias Mauri sunt. Super Numidiam Gaetu-   5
los accepimus partim in tuguriis, alios incultius uagos
agitare, post eos Aethiopas esse, dehinc loca exusta solis   6
75 ardoribus.

Igitur bello Iugurthino pleraque ex Punicis oppida et   7
finis Carthaginiensium quos nouissume habuerant populus Romanus per magistratus administrabat; Gaetulorum
magna pars et Numidae usque ad flumen Muluccham sub
80 Iugurtha erant; Mauris omnibus rex Bocchus imperitabat,
praeter nomen cetera ignarus populi Romani itemque
nobis neque bello neque pace antea cognitus. De Africa et   8
eius incolis ad necessitudinem rei satis dictum.

84

1   At Marius, ut supra diximus, cupientissuma plebe con-   84.1
sul factus, postquam ei prouinciam Numidiam populus
iussit, antea iam infestus nobilitati, tum uero multus atque
ferox instare, singulos modo, modo uniuorsos laedere,
5   dictitare sese consulatum ex uictis illis spolia cepisse, alia
praeterea magnifica pro se et illis dolentia; interim quae   2
bello opus erant prima habere, postulare legionibus

supplementum, auxilia a populis et regibus arcessere,

praeterea ex Latio sociisque fortissumum quemque, ple-

10 rosque militiae, paucos fama cognitos, adcire et ambiundo

cogere homines emeritis stipendiis secum proficisci.

Neque illi senatus, quamquam aduorsus erat, de ullo

negotio abnuere audebat; ceterum supplementum etiam   3

laetus decreuerat, quia neque plebi militia uolenti puta-

15 batur et Marius aut belli usum aut studia uolgi amissurus.

Sed ea res frustra sperata: tanta lubido cum Mario eundi

plerosque inuaserat. Sese quisque praeda locupletem fore,   4

uictorem domum rediturum, alia huiusce modi animis

trahebant, et eos non paulum oratione sua Marius adrexe-

20 rat. Nam postquam omnibus quae postulauerat decretis   5

milites scribere uolt, hortandi causa simul et nobilitatem,

uti consueuerat, exagitandi contionem populi aduocauit.

Deinde hoc modo disseruit:

85

1   'Scio ego, Quirites, plerosque non isdem artibus im-   85.1

perium a uobis petere et, postquam adepti sunt, gerere:

primo, industrios, supplicis modicos esse, dein per igna-

uiam et superbiam aetatem agere. Sed mihi contra ea

5   uidetur; nam quo pluris est uniuorsa res publica quam   2

consulatus aut praetura, eo maiore cura illam administrari

quam haec peti debere. Neque me fallit quantum cum   3

maxumo uostro beneficio negoti sustineam. Bellum parare

simul et aerario parcere, cogere ad militiam eos quos nolis

10   offendere, domi forisque omnia curare et ea agere inter

inuidos, occursantis, factiosos opinione, Quirites, asperius

est. Ad hoc, alii si deliquere, uetus nobilitas, maiorum   4

fortia facta, cognatorum et adfinium opes, multae cliente-

lae, omnia haec praesidio adsunt: mihi spes omnes in

15 memet sitae, quas necesse est uirtute et innocentia tutari;

nam alia infirma sunt. Et illud intellego, Quirites, omnium   5

ora in me conuorsa esse, aequos bonosque fauere—quippe

mea bene facta rei publicae procedunt—nobilitatem

locum inuadundi quaerere. Quo mihi acrius adnitundum   6

20 est uti neque uos capiamini et illi frustra sint. Ita ad hoc   7

aetatis a pueritia fui uti omnis labores et pericula consueta

habeam: quae ante uostra beneficia gratuito faciebam, ea   8

uti accepta mercede deseram non est consilium, Quirites.

Illis difficile est in potestatibus temperare qui per ambi-   9

25 tionem sese probos simulauere: mihi, qui omnem aetatem

in optumis artibus egi, bene facere iam ex consuetudine in

naturam uortit.

'Bellum me gerere cum Iugurtha iussistis, quam rem   10

nobilitas aegerrume tulit. Quaeso, reputate cum animis

30 uostris num id mutare melius sit. Si quem ex illo globo

nobilitatis ad hoc aut aliud tale negotium mittatis, homi-

nem ueteris prosapiae ac multarum imaginum et nullius

stipendi, scilicet ut in tanta re ignarus omnium trepidet,

festinet, sumat aliquem ex populo monitorem offici sui. Ita 11

35 plerumque euenit ut quem uos imperare iussistis, is sibi

imperatorem alium quaerat. Atque ego scio, Quirites, qui   12

postquam consules facti sunt et acta maiorum et Graeco-

rum militaria praecepta legere coeperint: praeposteri

homines, nam gerere quam fieri tempore posterius, re
40 atque usu prius est. Conparate nunc, Quirites, cum   13
illorum superbia me hominem nouom: quae illi audire aut
legere solent, eorum partem uidi, alia egomet gessi; quae
illi litteris, ea ego militando didici Nunc uos existumate   14
facta an dicta pluris sint. Contemnunt nouitatem meam,
45 ego illorum ignauiam: mihi fortuna, illis probra obiec-
tantur. Quamquam ego naturam unam et communem   15
omnium existumo, sed fortissumum quemque generosis-
sumum; ac si iam ex patribus Albini aut Bestiae quaeri   16
posset mene an illos ex se gigni maluerint, quid respon-
50 suros creditis nisi sese liberos quam optumos uoluisse?
Quod si iure me despiciunt, faciant item maioribus suis,   17
quibus, uti mihi, ex uirtute nobilitas coepit. Inuident   18
honori meo: ergo inuideant labori, innocentiae, periculis
etiam meis, quoniam per haec illum cepi. Verum homines   19
55 corrupti superbia ita aetatem agunt quasi uostros honores
contemnant; ita hos petunt quasi honeste uixerint. Ne illi   20
falsi sunt, qui diuorsissumas res pariter expectant, ignauiae uoluptatem et praemia uirtutis. Atque etiam, quom   21
apud uos aut in senatu uerba faciunt, pleraque oratione
60 maiores suos extollunt: eorum fortia facta memorando
clariores sese putant. Quod contra est; nam quanto uita   22
illorum praeclarior, tanto horum socordia flagitiosior. Et   23
profecto ita se res habet: maiorum gloria posteris quasi
lumen est, neque bona neque mala eorum in occulto
65 patitur. Huiusce rei ego inopiam fateor, Quirites, uerum,   24
id quod multo praeclarius est, meamet facta mihi dicere

licet. Nunc uidete quam iniqui sint: quod ex aliena uirtute   25

sibi adrogant, id mihi ex mea non concedunt, scilicet quia

imagines non habeo et quia mihi noua nobilitas est, quam

70   certe peperisse melius est quam acceptam corrupisse.

    'Equidem ego non ignoro, si iam mihi respondere   26

uelint, abunde illis facundam et conpositam orationem

fore. Sed in maxumo uostro beneficio quom omnibus locis

meque uosque maledictis lacerent, non placuit reticere, ne

75   quis modestiam in conscientiam duceret. Nam me quidem   27

ex animi mei sententia nulla oratio laedere potest, quippe

uera necesse est bene praedicent, falsa uita moresque mei

superant. Sed quoniam uostra consilia accusantur, qui   28

mihi summum honorem et maxumum negotium inposuis-

80   tis, etiam atque etiam reputate num eorum paenitendum

sit. Non possum fidei causa imagines neque triumphos aut   29

consulatus maiorum meorum ostentare, at, si res postulet,

hastas, uexillum, phaleras, alia militaria dona, praeterea

cicatrices aduorso corpore. Hae sunt meae imagines, haec   30

85   nobilitas, non hereditate relicta, ut illa illis, sed quae

egomet plurumis laboribus et periculis quaesiui. Non sunt   31

conposita uerba mea: parui id facio. Ipsa se uirtus satis

ostendit: illis artificio opus est, ut turpia facta oratione

tegant. Neque litteras Graecas didici: parum placebat eas   32

90   discere, quippe quae ad uirtutem doctoribus nihil pro-

fuerant. At illa multo optuma rei publicae doctus sum: 33

hostem ferire, praesidia agitare, nihil metuere nisi turpem

famam, hiemem et aestatem iuxta pati, humi requiescere,

eodem tempore inopiam et laborem tolerare. His ego   34

95 praeceptis milites hortabor, neque illos arte colam, me

opulenter, neque gloriam meam, laborem illorum faciam.

Hoc est utile, hoc ciuile imperium. Namque quom tute per   35

mollitiem agas, exercitum supplicio cogere, id est domi-

num, non imperatorem esse. Haec atque alia talia maiores   36

100 uostri faciundo seque remque publicam celebrauere. Quis —   37

nobilitas freta, ipsa dissimilis moribus, nos illorum aemu-

los contemnit et omnis honores non ex merito, sed quasi

debitos a uobis repetit. Ceterum homines superbissumi   38

procul errant. Maiores eorum omnia quae licebat illis

105 reliquere, diuitias, imagines, memoriam sui praeclaram;

uirtutem non reliquere, neque poterant: ea sola neque

datur dono neque accipitur. Sordidum me et incultis   39

moribus aiunt, quia parum scite conuiuium exorno neque

histrionem ullum neque pluris preti coquom quam uili-

110 cum habeo. Quae mihi lubet confiteri, Quirites; nam ex   40

parente meo et ex aliis sanctis uiris ita accepi, munditias

mulieribus, uiris laborem conuenire, omnibusque bonis

oportere plus gloriae quam diuitiarum esse; arma, non

supellectilem decori esse. Quin ergo quod iuuat, quod   41

115 carum aestumant, id semper faciant: ament, potent, ubi

adulescentiam habuere, ibi senectutem agant, in con-

uiuiis, dediti uentri et turpissumae parti corporis; sudo-

rem, puluerem et alia talia relinquant nobis, quibus illa

epulis iucundiora sunt. Verum non ita est. Nam ubi se   42

120 flagitiis dedecorauere turpissumi uiri, bonorum praemia

ereptum eunt. Ita iniustissume luxuria et ignauia, pes-   43

sumae artes, illis qui coluere eas nihil officiunt, rei

publicae innoxiae cladi sunt.

'Nunc, quoniam illis quantum mei mores, non illorum   44
125 flagitia poscebant respondi, pauca de re publica loquar.

Primum omnium de Numidia bonum habete animum,   45

Quirites. Nam quae ad hoc tempus Iugurtham tutata sunt,

omnia remouistis, auaritiam, inperitiam atque superbiam.

Deinde exercitus ibi est locorum sciens, sed mehercule   46

130 magis strenuos quam felix; nam magna pars eius auaritia

aut temeritate ducum adtrita est. Quam ob rem uos,   47

quibus militaris aetas est, adnitimini mecum et capessite

rem publicam, neque quemquam ex calamitate aliorum

aut imperatorum superbia metus ceperit. Egomet in

135 agmine aut in proelio consultor idem et socius periculi

uobiscum adero, meque uosque in omnibus rebus iuxta

geram. Et profecto dis iuuantibus omnia matura sunt: 48

uictoria, praeda, laus. Quae si dubia aut procul essent,

tamen omnis bonos rei publicae subuenire decebat;

140 etenim nemo ignauia inmortalis factus est, neque quis-   49

quam parens liberis uti aeterni forent optauit, magis uti

boni honestique uitam exigerent. Plura dicerem, Quirites,   50

si timidis uirtutem uerba adderent; nam strenuis abunde

dictum puto.'

86.1–3

1   Huiusce modi oratione habita Marius, postquam plebis   86.1

animos adrectos uidet, propere conmeatu, stipendio,

armis aliisque utilibus nauis onerat; cum his A. Manlium

legatum proficisci iubet. Ipse interea milites scribere, non   2

5   more maiorum neque ex classibus, sed uti quoiusque

lubido erat, capite censos plerosque. Id factum alii inopia   3

bonorum, alii per ambitionem consulis memorabant, quod

ab eo genere celebratus auctusque erat et homini poten-

tiam quaerenti egentissumus quisque opportunissumus,

10   quoi neque sua cara, quippe quae nulla sunt, et omnia cum

pretio honesta uidentur.

❧ *Historiae*

2.70

1   At Metellus in ulteriorem Hispaniam post annum

regressus magna gloria concurrentium undique, uirile et

muliebre secus, per uias et tecta omnium uisebatur. Eum

quaestor C. Vrbinus aliique cognita uoluntate cum ad

5   cenam inuitauerant, ultra Romanum ac mortalium etiam

morem curabant, exornatis aedibus per aulaea et insignia,

scenisque ad ostentationem histrionum fabricatis, simul

croco sparsa humus et alia in modum templi celeberrimi.

Praeterea tum sedenti transenna demissum Victoriae

10   simulacrum cum machinato strepitu tonitruum coronam

capiti inponebat, tum uenienti ture quasi deo supplica-

batur. Toga picta plerumque amiculo erat accumbenti,

epulae uero quaesitissumae neque per omnem modo

prouinciam, sed trans maria ex Mauretania uolucrum et

15   ferarum incognita antea plura genera. Quis rebus ali-

quantam partem gloriae dempserat, maxumeque apud

ueteres et sanctos uiros superba illa, grauia, indigna

Romano imperio aestumantis.

Commentary

∾ *Bellum Catilinae*

Although the opening chapter of the monograph begins with the abstract antithesis between mind and body, Sallust swiftly applies this imagery to the concrete pursuit of *gloria* and *uirtus*. I paraphrase: "All men who are eager to outstrip the other living creatures ought to vie with all their might so that they not live their lives in silence, like herds naturally slaves to the belly. Rather, the power of mankind resides in both mind and body, the one in common with the gods, the other with beasts. So I think it all the more right to seek the glory of intellect, not force, since the life we live is short but memory extends as far as possible; for the glory of wealth and beauty shifts and shatters, but *uirtus*—prowess both on and off the battlefield—is brilliant and eternal." The earliest kings exercised either deliberation (mind) or action (body), but eventually the most successful empires were built by intellect. A good state needs both men of action and men of words to guarantee their reputation. Sallust argues that it is especially difficult to write of the deeds of others, because the writer can be accused of malice, resentment, or fabrication. Therefore, his first order of business is to justify his undertaking.

Sallust (re)turns to history, 3.3–4.5

Sallust entered public office with a youthful innocence only to find unscrupulous behavior, bribery, and profiteering. Led astray by ambition and embroiled in rivalry, he decided to retire from politics but did not wish to waste his time with meaningless hobbies. Instead he took up the worthwhile task of writing history. All ancient historians begin with a statement of purpose; according to Marincola (1997, 62), such personal statements of intention "present this 'private' decision as one with benefit to individuals and the state." For Sallust, the decision to write history is presented as an attempt to display his *uirtus* for the benefit of society, since participation in politics is no longer possible. See also Katz (1983).

3.3   **Sed** The conj. connects this paragraph to the previous, in which Sallust bemoans the difficulty of writing history, but with an adversative force that signals the biographical content of what follows.

adulescentulus With the diminutive in apposition to *ego*, Sallust appears self-effacing and can distinguish his (childish) past from the mature and sensible present in which he composes the monograph.

initio abl. of time used as adv., "in the beginning, originally, at first"

studio abl. of means with *latus sum*. *Studium* is the hallmark of the dedicated historian, but in youth, Sallust's *studium* was misdirected toward politics (*rem publicam*).

rem publicam Here the phrase *res publica* refers to the welfare of the state or the public good, but it can also refer to the body politic of Rome. Eventually *res publica*, sometimes printed as one word, comes to refer to the Republic, the form of government with annually elected magistrates and a Senate composed of former magistrates.

mihi dat. of disadvantage with the adj. *aduorsa*

fuere = *fuerunt*

Nam . . . uigebant The grammatical simplicity of this intransitive sentence is enhanced by its rhetorical complexity. The anaphora of the prep. emphasizes the triad in asyndeton; each abl. object contrasts with a nom. subject. According to Frazer (1961, 252), "*nam*-clauses help to create the brevity and speed of expresson for which Sallust is famous."

3.4–5   **Quae . . . uexabat** Sallust explains his youthful mistakes in two clearly marked concessive clauses that contrast his individual character (capable of change) with the common (and unchanged) character of others: *tametsi . . . tamen* and *quom . . . nihilo minus*.

3.4   **Quae** acc. pl. n. direct object of deponent *aspernabatur*. A rel. pron. often stands at the beginning of a clause to connect it with the clause that precedes.

tametsi introducing a concessive clause, answered by *tamen*

aspernabatur deponent

malarum artium gen. with *insolens*, "unaccustomed to evil practices"

ambitione abl. of means with *corrupta*, nom. sing. f.

3.5   **me** acc. object of *uexabat*

dissentirem subjunctive in a concessive clause introduced by *quom*, answered by *nihilo minus*

eadem qua abl. sing. f. with instrumental abls. *fama* and *inuidia*; *honoris cupido uexabat* is gapped, "harassed me with the same reputation and envy as it did the others." Also called ellipsis or brachyology; the reader must supply the missing elements to complete the syntax.

4.1   **Igitur** emphasizes the beginning of the longest sentence of the paragraph, in which Sallust finally turns to writing history after rejecting other, lesser occupations. In classical Latin, *igitur* is preferably the second word in the sentence (post-positive) but Sallust almost always uses it in initial position, perhaps imitating Cato and the earlier, fragmentary historians; thus, *igitur* at the beginning of a sentence has an archaizing effect.

ubi introduces *requieuit et . . . decreui*

animus Sallust's frame of mind (*animus*, cf. 3.4) changed *ex multis miseriis atque periculis* (abl. of cause), "after many woes and dangers"

mihi dat. of agent with pass. periphrastic, *habendam* (supply *esse*)

habendam supply *esse* for indirect statement, the subject is *aetatem*, "I decided the rest of my life must be held by me," i.e., "I decided I must hold the rest of my life"

non fuit consilium impers. expression, "it was not the plan," governs two transitive infinitives: *otium conterere, neque . . . aetatem agere*

agrum colundo aut uenando abls. depending on *intentum*, which is acc. sing. m. agreeing with *me*, unexpressed subject of *agere* (as Ramsey notes). It is surprising that Sallust would abjure hunting, since it was a popular sport among Roman elite. For example, according to Polybius 31.29.3–12, Scipio Aemilianus (consul in 147) was an avid huntsman; Pliny the Younger (*Ep.* 1.6) recounts that the historian Tacitus also enjoyed hunting. Sallust mentions Jugurtha's hunting prowess at *BI* 6.1.

seruilibus officiis in apposition to *agrum colundo aut uenando*

4.2 **incepto studioque** construe the word order thus: *regressus eodem incepto studioque a quo ambitio mala me detinuerat.* Sallust's original undertaking was the writing of history, interrupted by evil ambition that caused him to misapply his *studium*. He returns (*regressus*) with the same *studium* (*eodem*) to the task of writing history. We are left with the impression that his foray into politics was temporary; he was always an historian after all.

carptim . . . perscribere emphasizes his chosen method of recording Roman history selectively (monograph versus universal history, after the manner of Coelius Antipater, see Introduction, xxix). The compound *perscribere* suggests thoroughness; the separation of *carptim . . . perscribere* by the *ut* clause mimics the meaning of *carptim*, "in separate or disconnected parts." Allen (1966) views this as a prefatory statement of method for all of Sallust's works, not just the *BC*.

ut + indicative, "as"

quaeque nom. pl. n.

memoria abl. of specification with *digna*

eo magis *eo* abl. degree of difference, "more so"

quod conj., "because"

mihi dat. of possession with *animus*

a spe metu partibus abl. of separation; three nouns of increasing syllables in asyndeton. *Partes* for Sallust is a general term for the division of the Senate and people; it designates a split in the state between groups with different political agendas. While the term "party" may be expedient, it does not correspond to the modern sense of large-scale political party organization.

4.3   **Igitur** By repeating the conj. from 4.1, Sallust moves from the general circumstances of his return to history to the specific topic at hand: the Catilinarian conspiracy.

de Catilinae coniuratione The first mention of Catiline and the first use of the term *coniuratio* suggest a title for the work. The title is disputed because the manuscripts are inconsistent; however, the later authors Quintilian and Florus both refer to the *Bellum Catilinae*. Sallust uses the word *bellum* throughout the monograph, and so he may have titled the work as a deliberate reaction to Cicero's insistence that war was averted.

quam uerissume potero *quam* + superl., "as truthfully as I can." This is the first of three times in the monograph that Sallust professes to relate events to the best of his ability. His account of the so-called first Catilinarian conspiracy echoes the claim: *de qua quam verissume potero* (*BC* 18.2). He is limited by the uncertainty and obscurity of his evidence, and so the disclaimer reminds us that the ancient standards of historical veracity are markedly different from modern expectations. Likewise, in the comparison of the characters of Cato and Caesar towards the end of the monograph, he promises to relate the nature and habits of each *quantum ingenio possum* (see below 53.6). By the end of the work, however, we come to realize with Sallust that this degree of veracity is only as high as the historian's ability (*ingenium*) permits.

paucis supply *uerbis*

4.4   **facinus** while the word can have a neutral meaning, "deed, act, event, thing," most of the time it has a negative connotation in Sallust

in primis adv., "above all," "especially"

nouitate abl. of cause, final position for emphasis

4.5 **quoius** gen. agreeing with *hominis*, i.e., Catiline; for the connecting rel. pron., cf. *BC* 3.4

prius . . . quam tmesis, "before"

faciam subjunctive introduced by *prius . . . quam* expresses purpose or expectancy, "before I expect to begin my narrative"

The character of Catiline, 5.1–8

In his orations, Cicero had so thoroughly discredited Catiline that by the time Sallust writes, it was nearly impossible to cast him as anything but a villain. The tone and content of the passage are imitated by Tacitus some one hundred years later in his character sketch of the emperor Tiberius' nefarious praetorian prefect, Sejanus (*Ann.* 4.1). For a reconsideration of Catiline's character, see Wilkins (1994).

5.1 **L. Catilina** His full name is Lucius Sergius Catilina, although Sallust never refers to the *gens Sergia*; he simply uses *Catilina* throughout. According to Vergil (*Aeneid* 5.121), the *gens Sergia* was descended from the Trojan Sergestus.

nobili genere abl. of source with pple. denoting birth (*natus*)

magna ui abl. of description

et animi et corporis "of both mind and body." At the beginning of the monograph, Sallust explains that men differ from beasts by virtue of their intellect: *sed nostra omnis uis in animo et corpore sita est*, "But all our strength is located in mind and body" (*BC* 1.2). Catiline is a specific example of this general composition of *animus* and *corpus*, but his intellect is corrupt.

5.2 **Huic** dat. with *grata*

adulescentia invites comparison with Sallust's youth

bella intestina caedes rapinae discordia ciuilis asyndeton of four subjects, the first and last with adjs.; *grata* is n. pl. predicate adj., modifying all four nouns

5.3   **Corpus** The two sentences 5.3 and 5.4 begin with the words
corpus and *animus* so as to expand upon the phrase *et animi
et corporis* (above, 5.1). The result is an elaborate chiasmus.

inediae algoris uigiliae asyndeton of objective gens. with adj.
patiens

supra quam "more than"

quoiquam dat. with *credibile*. The adj. exonerates the historian (to a degree) from responsibility for the outlandish tales
he must tell.

5.4   **Animus** supply *est*. Sallust's *animus* matured as he rejected
political life and (re)turned to writing history, but Catiline's
animus is beyond rehabilitation.

audax subdolus uarius asyndeton. *Audax* echoes *audacia*
(3.3), one of the prevalent vices of the age; *subdolus* contrasts
with Sallust's claim to truthfulness (*uerissume*, 4.3); *uarius*
suggests fickleness as opposed to a uniformity of purpose.

quoius . . . lubet tmesis, "of whatever you please"

simulator ac dissimulator annominatio

alieni . . . sui n. sing. substantive adjs., objective gens. with
adpetens and *profusus*

satis . . . parum supply *erat*; chiasmus emphasizes the antithesis, as Ramsey notes

5.5   **inmoderata incredibilia nimis alta** acc. pl. n. substantive
adjs. in asyndeton

5.6   **Hunc** i.e., Catiline; object of *inuaserat*

rei publicae capiundae gerundive objective gen. with *lubido*;
capiundae is an archaic spelling

neque conj. connecting the two independent clauses *inuaserat*
and *habebat*

neque . . . quicquam pensi habebat For the idiom, *nihil pensi
habere*, "to regard as of no importance," see *pendo* in the Vocabulary. *Neque . . . quicquam* is the equivalent of *nihil*; *pensi*
is partitive gen. with *quicquam*, the direct object. The indirect

question serves as the object of the verb *habere*, "to consider," which takes a double acc., "He considered how he might achieve it [*id quibus modis adsequeretur*] . . . a matter of no importance [*neque . . . quicquam pensi*]."

id acc. sing. n., referring to *rei publicae capiendae*; construe as the object of *adsequeretur* in hyperbaton

adsequeretur subjunctive in indirect question introduced by *quibus modis*, "in what ways (how) he might achieve it"

pararet subjunctive in a proviso clause introduced by *dum*

5.7 **Agitabatur** *agitare* derives from *agere* + the iterative suffix *-ito* to denote repeated action; this intensive or iterative sense of the word is emphasized by its first position in the sentence

in dies distributive phrase used only with compar. or verbs of increasing or decreasing; "daily," "day by day"

inopia . . . conscientia abls. of means with *agitabatur*

rei familiaris personal or private property contrasts with the concept of *res publica*. The phrase is echoed in Augustine, *Confessions* 2.5.11: *propter inopiam rei familiaris et conscientiam scelerum*, "on account of lack of family fortune and guilt for crimes."

quae utraque *quae* is nom. sing. f. (instead of gen. pl.) by attraction, "each of which"

auxerat *augescere* derives from *augēre* + the incohative suffix *-sco* to denote the beginning of an action, but this special sense has faded. Incohatives are generally intransitive.

5.8 **Incitabant** transitive, supply direct object inferred from *animus ferox* in 5.7; for initial position, cf. *agitabatur*, 5.7 above.

diuorsa inter se "mutually opposed"

mala nom. pl. n., in apposition to *luxuria atque auaritia*

luxuria atque auaritia Sallust must admit that, although Catiline's personal character is faulty, he was also a victim of the times, influenced by the corruption of others. Sallust repeats the phrase *luxuria atque auaritia* at *BC* 12.2. He attributes the moral crisis at Rome to the destruction of Carthage in 146 (*BC* 7–10) and to Sulla's dictatorship (*BC* 11.4) and implies, in part, that contact with foreigners hastened the conditions that left Rome ripe for conspiracy. Often Roman historians will attribute causes to moral degeneration caused by luxury and greed, but their insistence on declining morality merely deflects attention from other possible causes for political conflicts, such as the inherent social and economic disparity at the root of a society so deeply divided along class lines.

uexabant cf. *uexabat*, 3.5 above

Catiline's sordid past, 15

In the intervening chapters 5.9–13, Sallust gives a truncated account of Rome's history: the legendary arrival of the Trojans, the expulsion of the kings, and the foundation of the Republic (6); expansion and conquest abroad, dissension and rivalry at home (7–9); the conflict with Carthage (10); the age of Sulla and its aftermath (11–13). In both form and content, the brief historical summary (characteristic of *breuitas*) is reminiscent of Thucydides 1.1–19, the so-called "archaeology" or narrative of ancient beginnings. The general character of Catiline in chapter 14 is complemented by a list of specific misdeeds.

15.1   **Iam primum** "to begin with," "first of all"

stupra *Stuprum* is a broad term that Roman writers used in a variety of contexts. Originally it meant disgrace in general, but later came to specify sexual disgrace, whether adulterous or forcible. It is a category of prosecution that denoted any sexual immorality, including adultery. The opposite of *stuprum* is *pudicitia*, the confinement of one's sexual activity to appropriate, conventionally sanctioned partners. In the broadest sense, *stuprum* violates the sexual integrity of freeborn Romans of either sex and in the case of men threatens the inviolability of the citizen male and the impenetrability of his body.

cum uirgine nobili her identity is unknown

cum sacerdote Vestae instead of *uirgo Vestalis*. As Ramsey notes, the six Vestal Virgins took a vow of chastity; punishment for breaking the vow was burial alive. This priestess is probably Fabia, half-sister of Cicero's wife Terentia, the date probably 73 (ten years earlier). Catiline and Fabia were tried and acquitted. See Cadoux (2005).

alia huiusce modi gen. of quality with demonstrative suffix *-ce*. Often Sallust will cap a list with an indef. n. pl. pron. as shorthand that conjures a sinister mood. *Alia* may allude to the murders that Catiline committed as a partisan of Sulla during his proscriptions (see Introduction, xvii).

contra . . . fasque as if to define *nefanda* by annominatio

15.2　**Postremo** introduces the most outrageous act of all

Aureliae Orestillae daughter of Cn. Aufidius Orestes, consul 71. See Marshall (1977). It is hard to resist seeing a play on the name Orestes, the son of Agamemnon and Clytemnestra. Orestes avenged his father's murder by killing his mother; he was absolved of the homocide by Athena. Catiline reverses the myth: instead of the son killing the parent out of vengeance, the parent kills the son out of lust (*captus amore*). Cicero alludes to the murder at *In Cat.* 1.14; the anecdote is also recounted by Valerius Maximus: "Overcome with a mad passion for Aurelia Orestilla, when he saw the only impediment to their marriage was his own son, who was his only child and already past puberty, he removed the boy by poison, and lit the marriage torch from his funeral pyre and to his new bride he offered his own childlessness as a gift" (*Memorable Deeds and Sayings* 9.1.9).

quoius possessive gen., "nothing beyond whose beauty did a good man ever praise"

bonus substantive adj.

quod conj., "because"

ea nom. sing. f., referring to Aurelia Orestilla, subject of *dubitabat*

nubere illi *nubere* commonly takes dat. of partner. *Nubere* is etymologically related to *nubes* ("cloud") and means "to veil oneself." According to Treggiari (1991, 163) the marrige ceremony hinges on the veiling of the bride.

priuignum Catiline's son by his first wife would have been Aurelia Orestilla's stepson.

adulta aetate abl. of description

pro certo creditur impers. pass. with infinitive, "it is believed for certain that he made his home empty." Credibility is strategically invoked just before the shocking abl. absolute, *necato filio*.

scelestis nuptiis dat. of purpose; *nuptiae* is derived from the verb *nubere* + *ia*, abstract noun suffix

15.3   **Quae . . . res** the entire preceding statement; for the connecting rel. pron., cf. *BC* 3.4

in primis cf. *BC* 4.4

causa . . . facinus maturandi "the reason for hastening the crime," i.e., the conspiracy

15.4   **dis hominibusque** dats. with *infestus*; note the repetition for emphasis of the prefix *in* in *inpurus . . . infestus*

neque uigiliis neque quietibus abls. of means; pl. suggests generality or repeated attempts

15.5   **Igitur . . . inerat** Catiline's inner state of mind is reflected in his outward appearance.

colos . . . oculi . . . incessus the triad is embellished by the chiasmus of noun-adj. of the first two elements and adj.-adv. of the third; *colos* is an archaic spelling of *color*

in facie uoltuque . . . inerat prep. *in* repeated in the compound *inerat*

Alleged human sacrifice, 22

In the intervening chapters 16–19, Sallust narrates the so-called first Catilinarian conspiracy. In the year 66, the consuls-elect were disqualified from office; Catiline offered himself as a candidate for consul but his application was rejected. In retaliation, a plot was supposedly formed to assassinate the consuls; however, Catiline, in his impatience, signaled the conspirators prematurely. The first Catiliarian conspiracy raises unanswerable questions; for an analysis of the evidence, see Seager (1964); Sallust concludes with a resignation: *De superiore coniuratione satis dictum*, "about the earlier conspiracy enough has been said," 19.6. This *satis dictum* has to be one of the greatest disappointments in Roman historiography, for Sallust most certainly has not said enough. But the apothegm allows Sallust to move the narrative forward in pursuit of *breuitas*.

In chapters 20–21, Catiline recruits conspirators with a speech and attracts as many followers as he can by promising to abolish debt, although according to Yavetz (1963), Catiline was no social reformer; he sought to win immediate support, not guarantee long-term change. Even so, Catiline compels the conspirators to swear allegiance, and he is rumored to have sealed the conspiratorial oath with human blood. By the time the story is recounted by Dio Cassius (ca. 164 to after 229 CE, a Greek historian of the Severan period), it has become much more grisly: "Catiline imposed the obligation of taking a monstrous oath. For he sacrificed a boy, and after administering the oath over his vitals, he ate these in company with the others" (37.30.3).

22.1   **Fuere ea tempestate** *ea tempestate*, abl. of time. Sallust often introduces contemporary views or evidence with a rel. clause of characteristic (cf. *BC* 14.7, 17.7); it allows him to distance himself from the ghastly story and criticize his sources without explicitly naming them. The outlandish rumors of "those at that time" contrast with Sallust's present (and sensible) point of view. Sallust can thus maintain credibility in spite of the shocking tale he is about to tell.

dicerent subjunctive in a rel. clause of characteristic introduced by *qui*, governs indirect statement, of which Catiline is the subject of the three transitive infinitives: *circumtulisse, aperuisse,* and *fecisse*

oratione habita abl. absolute refers to Catiline's speech in chapter 20 (not in this volume)

popularis acc. pl. m., "accomplices"

adigeret subjunctive in circumstantial *cum* clause, "when he caused the accomplices of his crime to take an oath"

circumtulisse the subject of the indirect statement is *Catilinam* in the first line of the passage

22.2   **degustauissent** subjunctive in circumstantial *cum* clause

consueuit impers. "it was customary" + complementary infinitive *fieri*

aperuisse . . . fecisse the subject is still *Catilinam,* 22.1

[atque eo dictitare fecisse] square brackets enclose words that the editor (Reynolds) thinks should be deleted. Ramsey retains the phrase but obelizes (encloses in daggers) *dictitare* to signify that it cannot be emended, since its subject would have to be the conspirators (not Catiline)

eo "in this way"

quo = *ut*

forent third person, pl., impf., subjunctive of *sum* in a substantive noun clause, object of *fecisse.* Sallust prefers *fore* to *esse.*

alius alii reciprocal prons. express concisely a double statement; *alii* is dat., "guilty of such a great crime, one with another"

22.3   **ficta** supply *esse.* Sallust attempts to identify the source of the defamation among those who sought to rescue Cicero from blame for executing the conspirators without a trial.

Ciceronis objective gen. After his consulship, Cicero incurred the enmity of the powerful and dangerous Clodius, who passed a bill stating that anyone who had executed a Roman citizen without a trial should be banished from Rome (see Introduction, xxi).

atrocitate abl. of means

eorum i.e., the Catilinarian conspirators whom Cicero executed

Nobis dat. of person judging, "in my opinion." In this insistence on thorough research, some have detected a hint of sarcasm toward Cicero, who in his orations repeatedly touts his exhaustive investigations of the conspiracy.

pro "in proportion to," or as Ramsey suggests, "considering," "in view of"

Cicero learns of the conspiracy, 23–24

The love affair between Curius and Fulvia allows for the transfer of critical information about the Catilinarian conspiracy. The failure of the plot depended on channeling the conspirators' secrets to the proper authorities. Fulvia is a critical link in the chain between the conspirators and the consul. See Pagán (2004, 41–46).

23.1   **Q. Curius** Quintus Curius, of senatorial rank, removed from the Senate in 70. He was mentioned at 17.3, capping a list of senators who participated in the conspiracy. According to Suetonius, *Life of Julius Caesar* 17.1–2, Curius was voted a sum of money because he was the first to betray the conspiracy. He attempted to implicate Caesar in the plot, but Caesar successfully defended himself by appealing to Cicero's testimony. Thus, Caesar prevented Curius from getting the reward.

haud obscuro loco litotes; for the abl. of source, see *BC* 5.1

flagitiis atque facinoribus a favorite alliteration, repeated at *BC* 14.1, 14.2, and 37.5. Alliteration makes phrases memorable and distinctive; here the repetition of the harsh-sounding *f* lends a tone of criticism to the phrase.

senatu abl. of separation

gratia almost always preceded by its object in the gen.

23.2   **Huic homini** instead of *in* + abl. as at *BC* 15.5

reticere . . . occultare . . . dicere . . . facere governed by *quic-quam pensi habebat*; for the idiom and its negation, see *BC* 5.6. Both Catiline and Curius abandon reason. The impression of complete disregard is enhanced by the rapid progression of the infinitives. The synonymous compound verbs *reticere* and *occultare* are transitive with direct objects expressed, while the antonym *dicere* together with the nonspecific *facere* is also transitive, but without an expressed object. The overall terseness derives from the increasingly general semantics and clipped grammar.

suamet enclitic -*met* for emphasis

23.3   **ei** dat. of possession

Fuluia, muliere nobili Her name is recorded by the later historians Appian (*Civil Wars* 2.3), Plutarch (*Life of Cicero* 16.2), and Florus (2.12.6), while Dio (37.29.5, 37.33.1) and Diodorus (40.5) do not use her name. The sources do not agree about her social status, here especially difficult to discern. By using *mulier*, a more pejorative term than *femina* or *matrona* (see Santoro-L'hoir 1992), Sallust may imply she is of lower class. Thus, the adj. *nobilis* would have to mean not that she was of a noble house, but that she was well known (presumably for her trade). On the other hand, *muliere nobili* may simply denote a woman of some social rank. It is possible that she was an agent of Cicero sent to gather intelligence from the conspirators. Her identity is otherwise unknown.

stupri on the semantics of the word, see above *BC* 15.1

quoi i.e., Fulvia, dat. with *gratus*; hyperbaton (the pron. belongs within the *cum* clause, but it is placed before the conj. for the sake of emphasis)

esset subjunctive in a circumstantial *cum* clause

inopia abl. of cause

glorians rare pres. pple. lends vividness to the scene

maria montisque . . . minari The alliteration moves from outlandish to sinister.

polliceri . . . minari . . . agitare complementary infinitives with *coepit*; at first Curius promises, then he merely threatens, finally he acts

ni = *nisi*

sibi dat. with *obnoxia*

foret subjunctive in dependent clause in indirect statement, introduced by *ni*, governed by the notion of threatening, "if she were not subservient to him"

ferocius compar. adv. followed by *quam*

23.4 **insolentiae** annominatio with *solitus*, thus suggesting Curius' unusual behavior

causa cognita abl. absolute. Apparently the increased physical abuse Fulvia suffered was enough to convince her that the Republic was in danger. Curius never told her anything explicitly; instead, his boasting (*glorians*) and his behavior (more rough than usual) appears to have been sufficient cause to deduce the conspiracy.

sublato auctore abl. absolute, "with her source removed," i.e., "withholding the name of her source." Fulvia protects Curius' identity.

quae quoquo modo "what she had heard and in what way (how)"

compluribus dat. indirect object with *narrauit*

23.5 **Ea res** refers to the preceding sentence: i.e., Fulvia's deduction (*causa cognita*) and divulgence (*compluribus narrauit*) of the conspiracy of Catiline (*de Catilinae coniuratione*)

in primis cf. *BC* 4.4

ad consulatum mandandum gerundive after the prep. *ad* expresses purpose

M. Tullio Ciceroni dat. with *mandandum*. Cicero is mentioned at *BC* 22.3 in the context of rumor and innuendo, but here his full name suggests the formality and dignity associated with the office of consul.

23.6　**nobilitas** derives from the adj. *nobilis*, "generally known or familiar." Those whose ancestors held a magistracy (especially the consulship) were *nobiles*, "known men" because they had the right to *imagines* (waxen death masks of their ancestors) that would have been worn by actors in ceremonial processions. Hence, the prominent display of *imagines* allowed these men and their families to be well-known to all. The abstract noun *nobilitas* denotes the aristocracy, the class of well-born citizens with the right to *imagines*. As the first in his family to achieve the consulship, Cicero obtained noble status. On *imagines*, see Flower (1996).

inuidia abl. of cause

quasi pollui pres. pass. infinitive. Although Sallust softens the metaphor of soiling or staining, he repeats it at *BI* 63.7, *quasi pollutus*. Apparently the defeat of a *nobilis* by an outsider or *nouus homo* in the late Republic was grounds for suspicion of electoral corruption or bribery.

aestuabat . . . credebant The collective noun *nobilitas* allows for the switch from sing. to pl.

homo nouos *-os* is archaic for *-us*. The term denotes a man who is first in his family to become a consul.

adeptus foret past general condition introduced by *si*, subjunctive in indirect statement

post predicate adv. as adj, "were behind in importance," "were secondary"

24.1　**comitiis habitis** abl. absolute. Elections were held in the summer of 64 for the following year, as per usual procedure. It would seem that Cicero knew about the brewing conspiracy even before he took office, but he was unable to take action until October of 63, some seventeen months later. It is possible that Sallust has rearranged the chronology of events, putting the affair of Fulvia and Curius before Cicero's election, in order to heighten suspense and magnify the danger. For chronology, I follow Hardy (1917).

popularis for the form, see *BC* 22.1

24.2 **in dies** see *BC* 5.7

agitare historical infinitive technically with nom. subject *furor*, but in essence Catiline is the subject. As Ramsey notes, *furor* is also the grammatical subject of *parare* and *portare* by zeugma (use of a word whose semantics apply to only one of the terms to which it grammatically belongs). The iterative *agitare* conveys Catiline's vigor.

pecuniam . . . sumptam mutuam "money taken up on loan," i.e., "money borrowed"

fide abl. of means or instrument "on his own or his friends' credit"

Faesulas for names of towns, acc. of place to which without a prep. Faesulae was an Etruscan town located on a hill five miles north east of modern Florence (see map). Sulla settled some of his veterans in the region; this led to unrest among the landowners who had been displaced.

Manlium Gaius Manlius, leader of discontented veterans of Sulla under whom he gained military experience and wealth

belli faciundi gerundive after *princeps*

24.3 **Ea tempestate** see *BC* 22.1

sibi dat. with *adsciuisse*

dicitur Catiline is the subject

mulieres a more pejorative term than *feminae* or *matronae*, see Santoro-L'hoir (1992)

ingentis acc. pl. m., modifying *sumptus*, derived from *sumere* + *tus*, denoting the action

stupro abl. of means

quaestui neque luxuriae dats. with *modum fecerat*; *neque* = *et non*, "had imposed a limit only just (*tantummodo*) to profit and not to luxury"

conflauerant Metaphors of fire and burning throughout the monograph adumbrate the fire and arson that Catiline plots against the city; cf. *aestuabat, BC* 23.6.

24.4   **eas** the *mulieres* who prostituted themselves

sollicitare . . . incendere . . . adiungere . . . interficere complementary infinitives with *posse*; subject *se*

seruitia urbana Slaves did not stand to benefit politically or economically from the conspiracy, and their participation posed a risk to the conspirators whom they could betray for rewards. It is more likely that slaves were fomenting revolt independent of the conspiracy, and Catiline was using to his advantage their unrest and the recent memories of the dreadful revolt of Spartacus. See Yavetz (1963); Shaw (1975); Bradley (1978); Hock (1988).

The portrait of Sempronia, 25

From degenerate women in general, Sallust moves to a specific example. The celebrated portrait of Sempronia depicts a woman who, although descended from the noble house of the Sempronii, is nonetheless thoroughly steeped in the very luxuries Sallust deprecated in the beginning of the monograph. Sallust singles her out as the epitome of the crumbling morals of the Republic; she personifies the growing distance between noble birth and ignoble life. Such a stereotypical portrayal renders her a one-dimensional figure in the text. Except for a brief mention at *BC* 40.5, she plays no significant role in the course of events and does not appear again in Sallust's monograph.

Because Sempronia's role is marginal, it is difficult to understand the purpose of this paragraph. Goodyear goes so far as to say that, "In a work clumsily planned as a whole Sempronia is the worst blemish" (1982, 275), but Boyd successfully argues that the paragraph is "both thematically appropriate to and structurally significant for the greater concerns of Sallust's monograph" (1987, 185). See also Cadoux (1980); Paul (1985).

It is also possible that Sallust may have had in mind Porcia, the wife of Brutus, who was privy to the conspiracy to assassinate Caesar in 44. Perhaps Sempronia's privileged position in the monograph is meant to draw attention to the differences between the two noble women and their involvement in a conspiracy. Sempronia's immodest behavior and her marital infidelity pale in comparison to Porcia's chastity and her loyalty to her husband. On Porcia, see Pagán (2004, 119–22).

25.1   **iis** abl. pl. f., referring to the *mulieres*, "among these"

uirilis audaciae The quality implied in *audacia* is properly a masculine trait; together with the adj. *uirilis*, there is no doubt that Sempronia oversteps the bounds of her gender. Having abandoned her proper femininity, she aspires to a masculine role.

25.2   **genere atque forma** abls. of respect with *fortunata*

uiro liberis asyndeton of abls. of respect with *fortunata*. Her husband, Decimus Junius Brutus, was consul in 77, and her son, Decimus Junius Brutus Albinus (not to be confused with Marcus Junius Brutus, see Introduction, xv), was legate of Caesar in Gaul and later one of his assassins.

satis suggests stability, also signals that Sallust, in his *breuitas*, need not say more about her family connections. The compars. scattered throughout the rest of the paragraph (*elegantius*, *cariora*, and *saepius*) give the impression of a woman who is over the top.

litteris Graecis Sempronia's knowledge of Greek literature gives her an air of sophistication, and yet paradoxically such knowledge was also regarded as suspect; cf. *BI* 85.32.

[et] . . . [et] square brackets enclose words that the editor (Reynolds) thinks should be deleted because Sallust prefers asyndeton

docta introduces three sets of skills, each expressed in a different grammatical structure: *litteris*, abl. of respect; *psallere et saltare*, infinitives; *multa alia*, acc. pl. n. The grammatical variation mirrors Sempronia's wide-ranging abilities.

probae dat. sing. f. with *necesse est*

25.3   **ei** dat. sing. f. with *cariora*, the antecedent is Sempronia

fuit sing. with nearest subject

parceret subjunctive in indirect question introduced by *an* (without *utrum*)

discerneres independent potential subjunctive introducing indirect question

peteret . . . peteretur subjunctives in result clause introduced by *ut*, anticipated by *sic*; supply *est* with *adcensa* (fire imagery continues). Enallage is a figure of exchange or substitution of one grammatical form for another; for example, "She goes to the opera *to see and be seen*." In this case, the shift from act. to pass. of the same verb suggests a universality, completeness, and totality of action. Enallage is used to amplify or build abundance of expression, but it can lead to hyperbole and exaggeration. Here, enallage underscores how utterly unseemly it was for a Roman woman to pursue men.

25.4 **prodiderat . . . abiurauerat . . . fuerat** asyndeton; *ea* (Sempronia) is the subject

conscia guilt is the trait of the conspirator: cf. Catiline's guilt *conscientia* at *BC* 5.7 and 15.4, and the conspirators' shared guilt *tanti facinoris conscii*, at *BC* 22.2

luxuria atque inopia abls. of cause

25.5 **posse** historical infinitive governing three complementary infinitives, as Ramsey notes

uersus facere, iocum mouere parallel word order (ABAB)

sermone abl. with the infinitive *uti*, modified by three adjs. joined by *uel*; the alternatives are not mutually exclusive. The parallel sentence structure illustrates Sempronia's *ingenium haud absurdum*, a litotes in contrast to her multifarious skills above.

inerat sing. with nearest subject. The verb expresses innate quality; cf. Catiline at *BC* 15.5 and Gabinius at 40.6

Catiline at Rome, Manlius in Etruria, 27.2–29

In chapter 26, Catiline, after losing his bid for the consulship in the summer of 63, turned to more desperate measures, including an aborted attempt on Cicero's life. He posts conspirators at key locations in the vicinity at Rome.

27.2   **Romae** locative

moliri Catiline (*ipse*) is the subject of this historical infinitive. Its rather generic meaning is spelled out by the next three tricola of infinitives. The first tricolon is composed of three transitive infinitives: *tendere, parare, obsidere*. The second is varied: *esse* (intransitive), *iubere* (transitive with acc.), *hortari* (transitive with substantive clause of indirect command). The infinitives of the third tricolon are intransitive: *festinare, uigilare, fatigari*. Furthermore, in the first and third tricola, two consecutive infinitives are followed by one in final position, while in the second tricolon, one infinitive is followed by two in a row. The result is an extended chiasmus that compensates for the asyndeton:

> *tendere, parare . . . obsidere*;
>
> *esse . . . iubere, hortari*
>
> *festinare, uigilare . . . fatigari.*

The first set of infinitives describe Catiline's actions, the second his behavior, and the third his physical prowess. Such deliberate artistry facilitates comprehension by guiding the reader through a seemingly protracted sentence to its satisfying resolution.

cum telo predicate prepositional phrase as adj., "armed"

intenti paratique essent subjunctives in indirect command governed by *hortari* introduced by *uti*, an older form of *ut* that is increasingly rare after Cicero but is used by Sallust for archaizing affect

dies noctisque acc. of extent of time

insomniis for Catiline's ability to withstand fatigue, see *BC* 5.3

27.3   **Postremo . . . officere** In this extraordinary periodic sentence, Catiline is the subject of both independent verbs (*conuocat* and *docet*), both pples. (*agitanti* and *questus*), and every infinitive except the last. *Docet* introduces three clauses of indirect statement, of descending complexity: (1) *se . . . praemisisse*; (2) *seque . . . cupere*; (3) *eum . . . officere*. The first indirect statement has two acc. objects: *Manlium . . . alios*, each modified with a clause expressing purpose. The second indirect statement has a complementary infinitive and a dependent conditional clause. Cicero is the subject of the third indirect statement; its simplicity gives impression that Cicero easily obstructs Catiline's elaborate plans.

agitanti transitive concessive pple. in the dat. with *procedit*, "nothing succeeded for him, although he provoked many things"

rursus Catiline had already summoned his conspirators for his speech (*BC* 20–21, not in this volume)

intempesta nocte abl. of time

per M. Porcium Laecam the prep. *per* is unusual; we would expect *ad*, "to the house of Marcus Porcius Laeca," which Cicero tells us was located on the street of the scythe-makers (*In Catilinam* 1.8). The meeting took place on the night of November 6.

27.4   **ibique** *-que* connects two independent clauses (*conuocat* and *docet*)

questus transitive pple. with cognate acc. *multa*, "complaining a good deal about their idleness"

parauerat Indicative instead of subjunctive in a dependent clause in indirect discourse expresses factual assertion, as Ramsey notes.

alios in alia loca The distributive prons. do not specify how many troops or precisely where they are stationed; rather, in their indefiniteness, "some in some places, others in other places," they inspire fear of the unknown, give a sinister impression of Catiline's activities, and add to the growing suspense of the story.

facerent subjunctive in rel. clause of purpose, "to start the war"

oppressisset plpf. subjunctive in a conditional clause in indirect statement standing for fut. pf. in *oratio recta* (as Ramsey notes), "if he should first have crushed Cicero"

eum marks a change in subject to Cicero, subject of *officere*

multum adverbial acc., echoing Catiline's many efforts and complaints (*multa de ignauia eorum questus*)

28.1 **Igitur** marks a clear transition from lengthy periodic sentence to a new sentence with two new subjects, Gaius Cornelius and Lucius Vargunteius

perterritis . . . ceteris abl. absolute

cum eo abl. of accompaniment

constituere = *constituerunt*

ea nocte paulo post abl. of time; *post* is adverbial

cum armatis hominibus abl. of accompaniment

salutatum supine of purpose with *introire*. The *salutatio*, or morning greeting, was a long-standing tradition in Roman society. Clients, free men who entrusted themselves to another and received protection in return, would go in formal attire (the toga) to their patron's house at dawn to greet him and escort him to work, both for protection and prestige. The number of clients, their wealth and status, were a testimony to the patron's own social standing. In return for their support, the patron regularly bestowed favors and benefits including food or money. The conspirators used the *salutatio* as an opportunity to gain entry to Cicero's home.

introire . . . ac . . . confodere infinitives after *constituere*

de inprouiso adverbial prepositional phrase, "unexpectedly," "suddenly," "without warning"

domi suae locative; the reflex. *suae* refers to Cicero, "at his own home"

inparatum modifies *Ciceronem*

28.2 **Curius** betrays the conspiracy through the agency of Fulvia

consuli dat. of disadvantage

inpendeat subjunctive in indirect question introduced by *quantum periculum*

28.3 **illi** nom. pl. m., i.e., the assassins

ianua abl. of separation with *prohibiti*

28.4-29 Manlius found followers among the discontented in Etruria. Once Cicero found out about the manifold dangers both within and outside Rome, he took the matter before the Senate, which declared a state of emergency and conferred exceptional powers upon the consuls.

28.4 **sollicitare** historical infinitive with three objects: *plebem*, *latrones*, and *nonnullos*

egestate simul ac dolore iniuriae abls. of cause with *cupidam* modifying *plebem*

nouarum rerum objective gen. with *cupidam*, "desirous for revolution." To the modern ear, "new" is neutral or positive; however, in Latin, *nouus* carries a neutral to negative connotation. In the words of Syme, "The Romans regarded novelty with distrust and aversion. The word 'novus' had an evil ring" (1939, 315).

quod conj., "because"

amiserat the subject is *plebs*

Sullae dominatione abl. of time; on Sulla's dictatorship, see Introduction, xvi–xviii

quoiusque generis gen. of quality

quorum with *magna copia*

quibus dat. indirect object, "for whom"

nihil relicui fecerat sing. verb with two subjects (*lubido atque luxuria*). *Reliqui* is technically a partitive gen., but the phrase is idiomatic, "made nothing of a remainder" = "left nothing"

29.1 **Ea** hyperbaton

nuntiarentur subjunctive in a *cum* circumstantial clause

quod causal clause explains Cicero's emotional distress; he is the subject of the two finite verbs: *neque . . . poterat neque . . . habebat*

priuato consilio abl. of means

longius temporal compar. adv.

quo consilio abl. of description, "of what intention"

foret subjunctive in indirect question introduced by the interr. adj. and the interr. pron. *quantus aut quo*; the subject is *exercitus Manli*, in hyperbaton

satis conpertum acc. sing. n., object of *habebat*, which takes a double acc. The indirect question is the other object, "nor did he consider enough ascertained how large or of what intention was the army of Manlius"

rem ad senatum refert a simple formula after the complex causal clause

rumoribus abl. of means with *exagitatum*, modifying *senatum*. The text reads *exagitatam* (modifying *rem*) but the sense of *exagitare*, "to arouse or excite" suits *senatum* better. Cicero is emotionally distraught by the uncertainty of the evil (*ancipiti malo permotus*, 29.1), but the Senate is stirred up by the rumors of the common crowd. Cicero delivered his first oration against Catiline to the Senate on November 7.

29.2 **quod** rel. pron. nom. sing. n., subject of *solet*; the antecedent is the subsequent clause

solet supply *fieri*

darent subjunctive in an indirect command; although *ut* is gapped, it is easily supplied in the context of the governing verb *decreuit*. For the idiom, see *opera* in the Vocabulary.

quid for *aliquid* (after *si*, *nisi*, *num*, and *ne*, the prefix *ali-* is dropped)

detrimenti partitive gen. after *quid*, "any harm"

caperet subjunctive in negative purpose clause introduced by *ne*. This is the formulaic expression of a *senatus consultum ultimum*; cf. *Hist.* 1.77.22 (not in this volume): *operamque dent ne quid res publica detrimenti capiat*, "let them devote their attention so that the Republic not suffer any harm"

29.3   **more Romano** abl. of manner

magistratui dat. with *permittitur*

maxuma modifies *potestas*, postponed for emphasis

parare ... gerere ... coercere ... habere asyndeton of infinitives in apposition to *potestas*; the first pair in parallel word order, the second in chiasmus

omnibus modis abl. of manner

domi militiaeque locative, "at home and on the battlefield," "at home and abroad." As my student Bob Lotfinia notes, *imperium* is command held abroad (*militiae*), while *iudicium* refers to civil legal proceedings conducted at home (*domi*), so that the locative phrase is in chiasmus with the objects of the infinitive *habere*.

nullius objective gen. with *ius*

consuli dat. of possession, "the consul has the authority for none of these things." The rhythm and sound of *populi iussu ... consuli ius* emphasizes the antithesis.

The Allobroges, 40–41

In chapter 30, the Senate sends out the consuls and praetors with armies against the conspirators outside Rome. Chapters 31–32 record the popular reaction to the manifest turmoil at Rome; fear grips the city. Cicero delivers his scathing indictment of Catiline, the first Catilinarian oration. In chapter 33, Catiline's accomplice Gaius Manlius sends instructions to Rome (on these instructions, see Williams 2000); Catiline departs. At chapters 34–35, Sallust is able to quote a letter of Catiline to another of his fellow conspirators.

In chapters 36–39, Sallust describes the political climate of Rome in the 70s and 60s and lists the kinds of men who joined Catiline. It is possible that Sallust draws on Cicero's second Catilinarian speech (2.8–10), in which Cicero also lists types of malcontents. Prominent in both Sallust and Cicero are the disaffected men from colonies established by Sulla. See Yavetz (1963).

After Catiline left Rome to muster forces in Etruria, he left Lentulus in charge. Lentulus enlisted the aid of Publius Umbrenus to solicit the participation of the Allobroges in the conspiracy. The Allobroges were a Celtic tribe in the province of Transalpine Gaul (see map), brought under Roman control in 121. As a businessman, Umbrenus was known to these people, and so he approached the ambassadors who had come to Rome.

40.1 **P. Vmbreno quoidam** dat.; Publius Umbrenus, a freedman probably executed with the other conspirators. His name suggests ancestors from Umbria. It may also derive from *umbra* meaning shade; thus he would be a "shadowy" figure. Elsewhere Sallust plays upon the etymologies of names: Turpilius at *BI* 67.3 and Sulla (felix) at *BI* 95.4.

dat Lentulus is the subject of the idiom *dare negotium alicui*, "to charge or commission a person (to)," followed by indirect command

requirat . . . inpellat subjunctives in indirect command introduced by *uti = ut*

possit subjunctive in a dependent conditional clause in indirect command

existumans archaic spelling, governs indirect statement, *facile eos . . . posse*. The pple. allows Sallust to shift point of view from his own authorial standpoint to the limited point of view of Lentulus. Thus, Sallust can posit intention and causation. The Allobroges are likely to participate in the conspiracy for two reasons: *oppressos* explains their immediate situation, and the *quod* clause their innate disposition.

aere alieno abl. of cause with *oppressos* (supply *esse*)

natura abl. of respect with *bellicosa*

esset subjunctive in a dependent causal clause in indirect statement

ad tale consilium the prep. *ad* is repeated in the compound pass. infinitive *adduci*; for such repetition of prep. and prefix, cf. *BC* 15.5 (*in . . . inerat*)

40.2   **quod** conj., "because"

ciuitatium gen. pl. f.; *ciuitas* is a mixed *i*-stem, that is, it assumes *i*-forms only in the pl.

notus erat . . . nouerat plpf. for simple past of the verb *noscere*; for the enallage of the pass. and act., cf. *BC* 25.3

eius antecedent *ciuitatis*

tantis malis dat. with *exitum*, supply *esse*

sperarent subjunctive in indirect question introduced by *quem exitum*, "what they hoped the outcome for such unfavorable conditions would be"

40.3   **queri . . . accusare . . . expectare** infinitives in indirect statement governed by *uidet*

auaritia magistratuum cf. 5.8. Provincial maladministration was a common complaint in the late Republic; see Introduction, xiii.

in eo i.e., in the Senate

auxili partitive gen. with *nihil*, "no help"

esset subjunctive in causal clause introduced by *quod*; the reason is attributed to the Allobroges and not given as Sallust's own opinion, as Ramsey notes

miseriis suis dat. with *remedium*, which is in apposition to *mortem*

inquit direct speech lends *enargeia*, or vividness to the narrative

effugiatis subjunctive in rel. clause of purpose

40.4   **Haec** acc. pl. n. in hyperbaton

orare historical infinitive, *Allobroges . . . adducti* is the subject

sui gen. with *misereretur,* subjunctive in indirect command introduced by *ut* and with verb of saying implied

nihil . . . esse indirect statement governed by *orare*

facturi essent subjunctive in rel. clause of result introduced by *quod* and anticipated by *tam asperum neque tam difficile,* as Ramsey notes

aere alieno abl. of separation

liberaret subjunctive in proviso clause introduced by *dum*

40.5 **Ille** Umbrenus

quod conj., "because"

foro dat. with *propinqua*

consili objective gen., "and not unfavorable for the plan"

<ab> diamond brackets indicate words that the editor (Reynolds) has added, because normally Sallust always uses a prep. with *absum,* although regular Latin usage does not require a prep.

40.6 **quo** = *ut* + subjunctive, a purpose clause, "in order that there might be more impressiveness in the conversation"; for *inesse* of innate characteristics, cf. Catiline at 15.5 and Sempronia at 25.5

sermoni dat. after *inesset*

Eo praesente abl. absolute

coniurationem aperit, nominat socios Umbrenus is the subject; he initiates the Allobroges into the secrets of the conspiracy. The chiasmus emphasizes the simplicity of the information; thus, the implication of *multos quoiusque generis innoxios* is the more sinister, for innocent men are named only to provoke the Allobroges' mounting unrest.

legatis dat. of possession

esset subjunctive in purpose clause introduced by *quo,* "in order that the courage of the ambassadors might be greater"

domum acc. of place to which, i.e., back to Gaul

41   The Allobroges decide to report the conspiracy to their patron, Quintus Fabius Sanga, who in turn informs Cicero. Cicero then advises the ambassadors to feign interest in the conspiracy and to lend their aid so that he may apprehend the conspirators.

41.1   **habuere** = *habuerunt*

   consili partitive gen. with *quidnam*

   caperent subjunctive in indirect question introduced by *quidnam*. In *oratio recta* (direct discourse), this would be a deliberative subjunctive. For examples of the rhetoric of desperation in the *BI*, see Dué (2000).

41.2   **In altera parte . . . at in altera** The Allobroges weigh their options, "On the one hand . . . on the other . . ."

   aes alienum, studium belli, magna merces in spe uictoriae The tricolon, in which the third element is modified by a prepositional phrase, is balanced by the alternatives *maiores opes, tuta consilia, pro incerta spe certa praemia*. The prepositional phrases expressing hope, the most insubstantial reason for joining the conspiracy, are arranged in chiasmus: *magna merces in spe uictoriae* (adj. / noun + prepositional phrase), *pro incerta spe certa praemia* (prepositional phrase + adj. / noun). The overall impression of rhetorical composure and equilibrium contrasts with the utter inability of the Allobroges to make up their minds, thus rendering the *fortuna rei publicae* (41.3) the more powerful force in the outcome of events.

41.3   **Haec illis uoluentibus** temporal abl. absolute, "while they were turning these things over in their minds"

   fortuna rei publicae Like Thucydides, Sallust is not inclined to attribute events to divine forces; where human reason or passion fail to explain an event, *fortuna* is invoked; see Scanlon (1980, 41–47). Sallust attributes salvation to *fortuna*—rather than to Cicero's (self-proclaimed) vigilance.

41.4   **Q. Fabio Sangae** dat. with *aperiunt*. Sanga was likely the descendent of Quintus Fabius Maximus Allobrogicus, who conquered the Allobroges in 121, and so a patron of the tribe. He is also mentioned in Appian *Civil Wars* 2.4. According to Dio 37.34.1, Cicero had many informants in his employment, but the name Sanga does not appear in the what is left of that textually corrupt paragraph.

patrocinio abl. after *utebatur*

plurumum archaic spelling; adverbial acc., "very much"

uti = *ut* with indicative, "as," "how"

41.5   **per Sangam** with the abl. absolute *consilio cognito*

legatis dat. with *praecepit*

simulent . . . adeant . . . polliceantur dentque subjunctives in indirect command introduced by *ut* and governed by *praecepit*; the first pair in parallel word order, the second in chiasmus

quam maxume *quam* + superl. denotes the highest possible degree, "as much as possible"

habeant subjunctive in purpose clause introduced by *uti*, governed by *dentque operam*; *manufestos* carries a sense of being caught red-handed, in the act

Cato and Caesar, 53–54

Catiline's supporters proceeded to cause disturbances in Gaul and Italy, while the conspirators in the city made careful plans. Meanwhile, Cicero's arrangements for obtaining evidence went according to plan; the Allobroges brought him written evidence, and Cicero was able to apprehend the conspirators at the Mulvian Bridge on the night of December 2 as they were attempting to join Catiline at night. Lentulus, Cethegus, Statilius, Gabinius, and Caeparius were put under house arrest, and initially public opinion was favorable toward Cicero, after he delivered his third speech *In Catilinam* on December 3. On December 5, Cicero summoned the Senate to deliberate punishment. Silanus proposed the death penalty, but Caesar spoke forcefully against it. Cicero delivered his fourth speech *In Catilinam* and was supported by Cato, who insisted that the gravity of the offence called for a severe example. Cato's proposal of the death penalty carried.

Sallust brilliantly handles the crucial debate, giving a very long speech to both Caesar (51) and Cato (52) and omitting the speech of Cicero altogether. The Senate decision affords Sallust the opportunity to contemplate the extent to which the achievements of Rome depend on the moral fiber of her statesmen through a comparison of the characters of Cato and Caesar (see Last 1948). In form and content, the passage invites comparison with the initial statement of purpose (3.3–4.5) and the character sketch of Catiline (5.1–8). Thus, by harkening back to the beginning, Sallust signals the impending closure of the monograph.

53.1   **adsedit . . . laudant . . . ferunt . . . uocant . . . habetur** historical pres. used for the pf. in a summary enumeration of past events. Note the asyndeton in the tricolon *laudant, ferunt, uocant.*

alii alios the expression denotes reciprocity, reinforced by the synchysis, "rebuking each other they called each other cowardly"

senati the gen. sing. in *-i* (as of the 2nd declension) allows for variation with the usual 4th declension *senatus*

53.2   **Sed** marks the beginning of a digression, cf. *BC* 3.3

mihi dat. with *forte lubuit adtendere*, "by chance it has been pleasing for me to observe"

domi militiaeque, mari atque terra The locatives express essentially the same notion, but with lexical variation that suggests the impressive scope of Rome's exploits and domination of both culture and nature.

sustinuisset "made possible," subjunctive in indirect question, introduced by *quae*; the clause is the object of *adtendere*

53.3   **Sciebam** impf. denotes the historian's continued efforts over a long period of time; cf. *constabat*, 53.4

contendisse . . . tolerauisse supply the subject *populum Romanum* from above 53.2

ad hoc adverbial (see *ad hoc* in the Vocabulary)

facundia . . . gloria abl. of specification (or respect) with *ante Romanos*, "above the Romans in eloquence . . . in glory"

Graecos . . . Gallos subjects of *fuisse* in parallel word order

53.4   **multa agitanti** The same phrase is used of Catiline at 27.3 and echoes the transitive pples. *mihi multa legenti, multa audienti* at 53.2 that denote the historian's increasingly complex method of collecting and evaluating material. The repetition of *multa* emphasizes thoroughness.

eoque factum uti *eo*, abl. of cause; *factum*, supply *est*, "and for this reason it happened that"

diuitias paupertas, multitudinem paucitas parallel word order of acc. and nom.

superaret subjunctive in substantive clause of result introduced by *uti*

53.5   **sua** with *magnitudine*

sicuti †effeta parentum† There are three possible solutions to the virtually unsolvable textual difficulty: (1) In some manuscripts, *parentum* has been emended to *parente* for an abl. absolute, "as when a parent is past child-bearing." (2) Yet *sicuti* with an abl. absolute is rare; therefore *effeta* may be nom. and *esset* must be supplied. Then *parentum* must emended to *partu* or *pariendo*, "just as if it (the *res publica*) were worn out by child-bearing." (3) It is also possible that a word dropped out, such as <*vi*> before *parentum* for an abl. absolute, "as if the vigor of their ancestors was worn out with child bearing."

tempestatibus Sallust activates the ship of state metaphor, "in many a storm-tossed sea"

Romae locative

uirtute abl. of quality or description; cf. *uirtute* and *moribus* 53.6

53.6   **memoria mea** abl. of respect. After reading (*legenti*, 53.2), interviewing participants (*audienti*, 53.2), and pondering (*agitanti*, 53.4), the historian is finally guided by memory to the conclusion, that two men in particular merit consideration.

fuere = *fuerunt*

Quos connecting rel. pron. best translated with the demonstrative "those"

res the subject matter at hand

obtulerat < *offero*; plpf. historical used for the pf.

fuit pf. historical used for the pres.

quantum ingenio possum cf. *BC* 4.3, *quam uerissume potero*. According to Batstone (1988, 306), the phrase means, "to the extent that my rhetorical talent allows me to be effective"

aperirem subjunctive introduced by *quin* governed by the negated expression *non fuit consilium*, "it is not the plan to pass over (them) in silence, but rather that I should explain . . ." For *non fuit consilium* with infinitives, cf. *BC* 4.1.

54   This is an exquisite exercise in antithesis, crafted with balance and equilibrium. The first sentence compares Caesar and Cato on equal footing. The next five sentences contrast them, using either parallel structures or grammatical variations. The last two periodic sentences are devoted to each individual. When an historian gives two alternatives, the second is usually meant to be considered more seriously than the first, thus giving the impression that Cato is the better man. Ancient biographers often included a synkrisis (a Greek word meaning "comparison") of two men. Plutarch (ca. 50–120 CE) wrote synkrises with his *Parallel Lives*; of the 23 pairs, 19 survive with comparisons. See Batstone (1988a) for an excellent discussion of the purpose and effect of the synkrisis.

54.1   **iis** dat. with *aequalia* denoting likeness

genus aetas eloquentia asyndeton. Although both were noble, Caesar belonged to the *gens Iulia*, an ancient patrician family that traced its descent back to Aeneas, while Cato belonged to the plebeian *gens Porcia*, which did not boast a consul until 195. In terms of age, Caesar was only five years older than Cato, apparently a negligible difference. In terms of *eloquentia*, Caesar was a proponent of the so-called Attic style of oratory, while Cato was a man of few words known for his laconic style. Thus, in the following sentences, Sallust describes Caesar with two or three words but Cato with only one.

alia alii "but some distinction was proportionate to one, other to the other." Once again, Sallust uses the distributive prons. for a shorthand; cf. *BC* 27.4. The sentence begins and ends with dats. depending on adjs. (*iis . . . aequalia* and *par . . . alii*).

54.2   **beneficiis ac munificentia . . . integritate** abls. of cause

Ille . . . huic "the former . . . to the latter"

mansuetudine et misericordia abls. of cause. We need not assume that Sallust is deliberately avoiding the term *clementia* because it was indicative of tyrants who lorded power over enemies by ostentatiously pardoning them. First, the word *clementia* is rare in Sallust (only at *BI* 33.4 and *Hist.* 1.55.1). Second, Konstan (2005) has demonstrated that *clementia* was a virtue in Caesar's day, not a gesture of tyranny. Third, in the *De Clementia* (written in 54 or 55 CE for the emperor Nero), Seneca the Younger uses *mansuetudo* (gentleness) as a synonym for *clementia* (Braund 2009, 243). He labors to distinguish *misericordia* (pity) as a defective form of *clementia*, probably because it is so often conflated (as here). Sallust opts for the alliteration of *mansuetudine et misericordia* so as to paint Caesar with two words, Cato with one (*seueritas*).

54.3   **dando subleuando ignoscundo . . . nihil largiundo** abls. of means

miseris . . . malis dats. of advantage and disadvantage

54.4   **in animum induxerat** idiomatic, "to form an intention," governs the infinitives *laborare, uigilare* in asyndeton; note the repetition of the prep. *in* in *induxerat*

intentus modifies *Caesar,* takes the dat. *negotiis*

sua supply *negotia,* acc. pl. n. object of *neglegere*

neglegere . . . denegare transitive historical infinitives

dono abl. of specification with *dignum*

magnum imperium, exercitum, bellum nouom asyndeton; chiasmus of adjs. and nouns with *exercitum* as central agent for achieving both *imperium* and *bellum*

posset potential subjunctive in purpose clause introduced by *ubi*; the only subjunctive verb in the paragraph, "when his virtue could (potentially) stand out conspicuously"

54.5 **Catoni** dat. of possession

studium cf. Sallust's *studium* for politics and writing history, above *BC* 3.3 and 4.2

54.6 **non diuitiis . . . abstinentia** abls. of respect with *certabat*, "he vied not in terms of wealth with the wealthy, nor in terms of partisanship with partisans . . ." Chiasmus and annominatio (*diuitiis, diuite; factione, factioso*) emphasize the sharp contrast between the two vices Cato eschewed with three virtues he esteemed, "but (he vied) with the energetic in terms of virtue, with the modest in terms of decency, with the blameless in terms of restraint"

quo minus . . . eo magis abls. of degree of difference, "the less . . . the more . . ."

Catiline's last stand, 60–61

Once the Senate consented, the five prisoners were immediately executed at Rome. Meanwhile, Catiline formed two legions and joined Manlius. The other consul, Antonius, pursued Catiline through the mountains on the border of Gaul. Once Catiline learned that the conspiracy had been betrayed, support waned. Catiline stopped at Pistoria (north of Faesulae, see map) and was shut in by Antonius; there he decided to risk battle. At the last minute, Antonius fell ill and put Marcus Petreius, a praetor and legate, in command.

60.1 **omnibus rebus exploratis** abl. absolute

tuba abl. of means

cohortis acc. m. pl.

idem acc. sing. n., artfully placed between *iubet* and *facit*, so that the action of the enemy army mirrors the action of Petreius

60.2   **eo** adv. with impers. pass. of intransitive *ventum est*, "After they arrived there"

concurrunt . . . omittunt . . . geritur tricolon in asyndeton, pres. tense for *enargeia* (vividness)

60.3   **pristinae uirtutis memores** Sallust shifts point of view, from the standpoint of the narrator to the limited point of view of the *ueterani*; the narrative interest shifts from the loud battle to the silent thoughts of the soldiers, which Sallust can only infer. Thus, the mention of *pristina uirtus* is an obtrusion that allows Sallust to bring forward his major theme at the most emotional moment of the monograph.

instare . . . resistunt . . . certatur another tricolon in asyndeton, to balance 60.2, but for variation, a historical infinitive, a verb with an expressed subject, and an impers. verb

60.4   **Catilina** subject of six historical infinitives that describe his increasing involvement in the battle, from general actions to specific. As Ramsey notes, at first Catiline tries to manage the entire field (*uorsari, succurrere*) and to reinforce the army (*arcessere*); but then he must see to everything, even the details (*omnia prouidere*). He ends up joining the fray and finally slaying men himself (*pugnare, ferire*). The result is that Catiline starts the battle as general, but eventually becomes a soldier. There is a sense that he is increasingly isolated.

exequebatur With this finite verb (in contrast to the six historical infinitives), Catiline performs the duties of soldier and commander (*strenui militis et boni imperatoris*, parallel word order), in chiasmus with the infinitives above.

60.5   **Petreius** hyperbaton, subject of *uidet*

contra ac ratus erat "otherwise than he had reckoned," i.e., Petreius expected Catiline to put up a better fight, and so he acted immediately on this perceived vulnerability

cohortem praetoriam an elite bodyguard assigned to a general

in medios hostis . . . alibi . . . utrimque ex lateribus The adverbial expressions of place give the impression that Petreius had the entire battlefield covered.

60.6   **Manlius** Unlike Catiline, who attempted everything in battle, Manlius and his troops simply fall, although they were fighting in the front.

60.7   **<Catilina>** diamond brackets indicate that the editor (Reynolds) has added *Catilina* so as to indicate the change of subject

fusas copias seque . . . relicuom chiasmus

memor generis atque pristinae suae dignitatis The shift in point of view continues the isolation of Catiline; at the hottest moment of his fighting, he is alone in his thoughts. Unlike the *ueterani*, he is not mindful of *uirtus* in the service of the *res publica*, but of his own personal rank and dignity.

61   The monograph ends with an aftermath narrative, a picture of the battlefield strewn with corpses. The field is inspected by the survivors, who come to bury the dead. The aftermath is part of the transition from war's violent disruption to relief and equilibrium. The scene necessarily looks backward and recreates the battle in the mind's eye, but it also looks forward to the more permanent results for the winners and the losers of the battle. Other aftermath narratives in Latin literature include Livy 22.51.5–9; Tacitus, *Ann.* 1.61–62, *Hist.* 2.70; Lucan 7.787–846; Silius Italicus 10.449–53; Statius, *Thebaid* 12.1–49. On aftermath narratives, see Pagán (2000).

Fowler (1997, 133–35) compares the end of the *Bellum Catilinae* to the end of Lucretius *De Rerum Natura*, the plague of Athens (drawn from Thucydides): both works employ *enargeia* (vividness); both end with visions of heaps of corpses strewn over a wide area; in both, the catastrophe strikes the civic sphere; both emphasize grief; both leave an open-ended, inconclusive feeling. Thus, it appears that Lucretius

(99–55), a contemporary poet who lived during the reign of Sulla and the Catilinarian conspiracy, provided some inspiration for Sallust.

61.1 **confecto proelio** temporal abl. absolute sets the aftermath narrative apart from the rest of the monograph

cerneres potential subjunctive in past time. With another shift in point of view, Sallust now brings the reader to the battlefield. The rest of the paragraph (and monograph) will be purely descriptive, but Sallust will draw inferences from the remains of the battlefield so as to recreate the battle in the mind's eye. Poets use the verb *cernere* to introduce *ekphrases* or ornate descriptions of works of art (e.g., the shield of Aeneas: *cernere erat, Aen.* 8.676).

fuisset subjunctive in indirect question introduced by *quanta . . . quantaque*

61.2 **quem** with *locum*

uiuos nom. sing. m.

pugnando abl. of means

eum with *locum*, "which place . . . that place"

amissa anima abl. absolute

61.3 **quos medios** "whom, in the middle, the praetorian cohort had scattered"

paulo abl. of degree of difference with compar. adv. *diuorsius*

aduorsis uolneribus Even though they were conspirators fighting against the *res publica*, Catiline's soldiers still displayed the requisite courage by facing the enemy in death. With this detail, Sallust can yet again register moral approbation.

61.4 **uero longe a suis** *suis*, abl. pl. m., substantive, "indeed far from his own men," continuing the isolation of Catiline

repertus est with *cerneres*, 61.1, another verb of visual perception

spirans Catiline hovers between life and death; the pple. conveys this marginal status with pathos. *Spirare* is the root of *conspiratio*, "to breathe together, to conspire," but here, Catiline, no longer in the company of his fellow conspirators, gasps his last breath alone.

ferociamque the *-que* connects the two pples., the intransitive *spirans* and the transitive *retinens*

uiuos nom. sing. m., cf. 61.2. Catiline is completely isolated as he alone wavers in the no-man's-land between life and death. He thus becomes a symbol of the body politic, representing the intermediate state of the Republic, gasping its last.

61.5   **ex omni copia** from Catiline's entire force

ingenuos nom. sing. m., "freeborn citizen." By using this word to describe the army of Catiline, Sallust reminds the reader that this was a battle of Romans against Romans. The pointed use of this adj. suggests that non-freeborn men may have fought on Catiline's side, but their low status excludes them from historical record. See Bradley (1978).

61.6   **ita** points back to 61.5, "in this way," i.e., by being captured neither in battle nor in flight, so as to negate *pepercerant*, "in this way, all spared their own lives and the lives of the enemy equally," which is to say, they spared none.

61.7   **exercitus populi Romani** Sallust next describes the disposition of the Roman army

Neque . . . laetam aut incruentam uictoriam The military strife is ended, but the Roman army is only beginning to realize the high price it paid.

strenuissumus quisque *quisque* is used idiomatically with superl., "all the most energetic"

aut . . . aut coordinates the intransitive verbs *occiderat* and *discesserat* in chiasmus

in proelio mirrors 61.5, the location of Catiline's troops in battle. The position of the bodies thus indicates the course of events, making it possible to recreate the battle in the mind's eye.

61.8   **Multi** hyperbaton, subject of *processerant*

uisundi aut spoliandi gratia states the purpose of the soldiers' return to the battlefield; *uisundi*, another verb of visual perception. In the immediate aftermath, survivors collect their dead in an intermediate step between war and peace, between conflict and resolution.

uoluentes nom. pl. m., transitive

amicum . . . hospitem . . . cognatum The relationships become increasingly more familiar, from friend, to guest, to relative.

alii, pars variation, "some, others"

cognoscerent subjunctive in rel. clause of characteristic

61.9 **Ita** introduces the *epiphonema*, or the concluding remark after a long train of thought, for an emotive, summarizing effect

laetitia, maeror, luctus atque gaudia Looking back, the survivors (and the reader) see the danger Catiline posed to the state; looking forward, they see the safety to which they are only just now delivered. In this intermediate state, the monograph ends with a chiastic flourish of emotions wavering between joy and grief. The antithesis of emotions is understandable, given that the enemies were actually Roman citizens. But it also suggests the precarious political condition of the Republic—not only in 63, but in Sallust's own day.

ꙮ *Bellum Iugurthinum*

The preface of the *BI* clearly echoes the preface of the *BC*. Sallust reiterates the distinction between mind and body, the preference for the former, and the importance of history writing (chapters 2–4), with one critical difference. The first paragraph emphasizes the potential of human nature for *uirtus*: "Wrongly humankind complains about its nature, that it is weak and brief and ruled by chance rather than prowess. For on the contrary upon reconsideration, you would find that there is nothing greater nor more outstanding, and that neither stamina nor time is lacking but rather the force of man's nature" (*BI* 1.1–2). This reformulation suggests an evolution of Sallust's thoughts about the complex notion of *uirtus*. In chapter 5, Sallust announces and justifies his topic before summarizing the prehistory and causes of the war.

The character of Jugurtha, 6–7

When King Masinissa died in 148 in the client kingdom of Numidia, on the border of the Roman province of Africa, Scipio Aemilianus divided rule among the king's three sons. Of these, Gulussa and Mastanabal died, leaving Micipsa sole heir. Micipsa adopted his brother Mastanabal's illegitimate son Jugurtha, but also had two sons of his own, Adherbal and Hiempsal. Jugurtha's strength and charisma alarmed Micipsa, who feared for his and his sons' position. In an attempt to rid himself of the young Jugurtha, Micipsa sent him to help Scipio Aemilianus in Spain (134–133); however, the plan failed and Jugurtha only proved himself the more competent in war and capable of securing favor.

6.1   **Qui** connecting rel. pron., i.e., Jugurtha

ubi primum "as soon as"

uiribus . . . ingenio abls. of specification in chiasmus with adjs. *pollens* and *ualidus*

decora facie abl. of description

multo abl. of degree of difference, usually with compar., here with superl.

luxu contracted form of the dat. *luxui*, indirect object

corrumpendum gerund of purpose

equitare iaculari . . . certare . . . esse . . . agere . . . ferire . . . facere . . . loqui Jugurtha is the subject of these historical infinitives. Numidians were famous in the Roman world for their cavalry. The rather innocent pastimes of horsemanship, athletics, and hunting build not only physical prowess but also character, for Jugurtha is above all modest about his achievements. Given the prominence of hunting in this description, Sallust's personal rejection of hunting (*BC* 4.1) is all the more conspicuous.

gloria abl. of respect

anteiret subjunctive in a concessive clause introduced by *quom*, answered by *tamen*

omnibus dat. with *carus*

leonem collective sing.

aut "or at least," corrects preceding statement, "first or among the first"

[et] square brackets enclose words that the editor (Reynolds) thinks should be deleted because Sallust prefers asyndeton

6.2 **Quibus rebus** connecting rel. pron., abl. of cause

initio cf. *BC* 3.3

existumans the pple. shifts point of view from the narrator (Sallust) to the inner thoughts of Micipsa, whose motives are altogether probable: this is *inuentio* at its best

uirtutem Jugurtha exhibits the preeminent Roman value of *uirtus*, military excellence that gains victory in battle.

regno suo gloriae "for a glory to his own kingdom," "the glory of his kingdom," "his kingdom's glory." *Gloriae*, dat. of purpose + *regno suo*, dat. of pers. reference, is predicated with the verb *fore*. The predicative dat. is also called double dat. Only about two hundred words in Latin are used in the double dat., and it is worth becoming familiar with the general semantic ranges that admit this construction. For example, the double dat. often expresses notions of help, anxiety, loss, grief, ruin, or the opposite extremes of honor, gain, boon, and glory. Furthermore, the dats. are rarely accompanied by adjs. other than those of quantity. Thus, the general formula makes the double dat. an easily recognizable construction: dat. of purpose (usually the notions listed above) + dat. reference (usually the person affected) + *esse*. The construction is less common in prose writers after Livy, but Sallust makes masterful use of its concision and elegance.

My students suggested possible approximations in English: "She is the apple of her father's eye," and "She is the bane of his existence." The positive and negative metaphors of purpose ("apple" and "bane") and the person affected, also metaphorically expressed ("her father's eye" and "his existence") are connected with the verb "is." These distinctly English idioms, like the double dat. in Latin, resist literal translation.

exacta sua aetate et paruis liberis abl. absolute without a pple. (Latin lacks the pres. pple. of *esse*), "his own age being far advanced and his children small"

intellegit historical pres. for pf.

negotio a synonym for *re*

permotus another pple. shifting point of view so as to attribute causes to Micipsa's emotional state

uoluebat impf. denotes repeated action, "he kept on turning many things over in (with) his mind." Although the expression is poetic, the substance of Micipsa's thoughts are probable; the final position of the finite verb is more forceful than the embedded pples. *existumans* and *permotus*.

6.3 **Terrebat** first in sentence for emphasis, sing. to agree with the first two of the individual subjects: *natura, opportunitas*, and *studia*, a tricolon of ascending complexity. With the back-to-back verbs, Sallust moves from Micipsa's emotional turmoil (*uoluebat*) to its cause. The homonymous endings (homoeoteleuton) of the third person sing. impf. indicative act. create equality of form, sound, and rhythm that binds the two sentences together while simultaneously emphasizing the overt differences in subject and meaning.

imperi objective gen. with *auida*, which modifies *natura*

ad explendam animi cupidinem gerundive with *ad* expressing purpose

aetatis subjective gen. with *opportunitas*, "the opportunity of (or afforded by) his own (old) age and his children's (young) age"

quae the antecedent is *opportunitas*

spe abl. of means

ad hoc adverbial; cf. *BC* 53.3

in Iugurtham "toward Jugurtha," i.e., in his favor

ex quibus the antecedent is *Numidarum*, "from whom"

dolis abl. of means

interfecisset subjunctive in conditional clause introduced by *si*, in the implied indirect discourse of Micipsa's thought

qua for *aliqua* modifying *seditio*

seditio aut bellum i.e., either domestic or foreign. *Seditio* is a rebellion that arises within the state and can refer to either civil or military insurrections.

oriretur subjunctive in fear clause introduced by *ne* and governed by *anxius erat*

7.1   **circumuentus, ubi** This periodic sentence begins with a pple. followed by a temporal clause (*ubi uidet*). The next periodic sentence (7.2) contains a temporal clause (*quom . . . mitteret*) followed by a pple., *sperans*. Thus, the chiastic arrangement of *circumuentus, ubi . . . quom . . . sperans* closely binds these two sentences together. The word order within the temporal clauses is also calculated for balance. In the *ubi* clause of 7.1, the verb *uidet* is in first position; in the *quom* clause of 7.2, the verb *mitteret* is in last position. To offset this balance, of course, *uidet* is indicative, while *mitteret* is subjunctive.

uidet historical pres. for pf.

neque per uim neque insidiis *uariatio*, prepositional phrase + abl. of means

popularibus dat. with *acceptum*; the word means "accomplices" at *BC* 22.1 and *BC* 24.1, but here, "to his countrymen"

manu promptus et adpetens gloriae *manu*, abl. of instrument, *gloriae* objective gen., pples. in chiasmus, "keen for a fight and desirous of glory"

eum obiectare . . . fortunam temptare parallel word order

periculis dat. with *obiectare*

eo modo abl. of manner, "in this way"

7.2   **bello Numantino** abl. of time, "in the Numantine war." Numantia, a town in Spain (see map), declared war against Rome in 143; though outnumbered by the Romans, the Numantines held out for ten years, defeated several generals, and captured the consul C. Hostilius Mancinus in 137. Numantia was captured and destroyed in 133 after a siege of fourteen months by Scipio Aemilianus Africanus, who had captured Carthage in 146. In 132 he acquired the honorary name "Numantinus."

mitteret subjunctive in a circumstantial clause introduced by *quom*

ostentando . . . saeuitia abls. of means with *occasurum* (supply *esse*) which is fut. infinitive with *sperans*; *uariatio* of gerundive and substantive

praefecit Numidis supply *eum*, i.e., Jugurtha, "put him in charge of the Numidians"

7.3   **longe aliter ac** "far otherwise than," after words of difference or likeness *ac* = *atque* means "than" or "as"

7.4   **inpigro atque acri ingenio** abl. of description

naturam P. Scipionis . . . et morem hostium acc. direct objects of *cognouit*, in parallel word order

Romanis dat. governed by *imperator erat* = *imperabat*

labore . . . cura . . . parendo . . . eundo abls. of means. The *uariatio* of substantives and gerundives reverses and doubles the order of 7.2 above, suggesting that Jugurtha's abilities reverse and outstrip Micipsa's sinister plans.

modestissume *modestus* used of soldiers is the technical term for discipline, "by obeying most strictly"; on military discipline in the Roman army, see Phang (2008).

periculis dat. with *obuiam eundo*, "by facing up to dangers"

breui = *in breui tempore*

nostris dat. with *carus*, i.e., to the Romans

Numantinis maxumo terrori on the double dat., see *BI* 6.2. Note the characteristics of the construction: dat. of pers. reference (*Numantinis*) + dat. of purpose in a negative semantic range with an adj. of quantity (*maxumo terrori*) + *esset*. The grammatical variation emphasizes the difference between Jugurtha's admiration among the Romans (*nostris uehementer carus*) versus his formidable reputation among the Numantines.

esset subjunctive in a result clause introduced by *ut* and anticipated by *tantam*

7.5   **quod** supply *id*, "that which." The antecedent of the rel. pron. is the following clause.

in primis cf. *BC* 4.4, especially emphatic with superl.

et proelio . . . solet The remarkable word order of this sentence is not only aesthetically pleasing, but it facilitates comprehension. The chiasmus in the main independent clause is centered on the perfectly poised verb *erat*. The rel. clause explains why Jugurtha's ability to balance these two character traits ("energetic in war and wise in council") is especially difficult to achieve. Within the rel. clause, the anaphora of *alterum . . . alterum* emphasizes a second chiasmus, for *prouidentia* is the result of being *bonus consilio*, while *audacia* is the result of being *proelio strenuos*.

proelio . . . consilio abls. of specification

strenuos nom. sing. m., archaic spelling

alterum . . . alterum nom. sing. n. subjects of *solet*

ex prouidentia . . . ex audacia abls. of cause

timorem . . . temeritatem acc. sing. direct objects of *adferre*

plerumque pleonastic (needless with *solet*). Such fullness of expression contrasts conspicuously with Sallust's characteristic concision.

7.6   **imperator** i.e., Scipio

per Iugurtham Scipio used Jugurtha for difficult missions.

agere . . . habere . . . amplecti historical infinitives, Scipio is the subject

magis magisque . . . in dies cf. *BC* 5.7

quippe quoius *quippe* with a rel. pron. introduces a causal clause, "since"; *quoius*, "of his"

neque . . . frustra litotes of the coordinating conj. *neque* with the predicate adv. *frustra* make this a particularly compact causal clause, "since no advice nor any undertaking of his was in vain"

erat Sallust generally uses the indicative instead of subjunctive in causal clauses introduced by *quippe*

7.7   **Huc adcedebat** "to this (i.e., to Jugurtha's virtues) was added." Technically the sing. verb has two subjects, *munificentia animi et ingeni sollertia*, but chiasmus binds them in a single sense unit. The intransitive *adcedere* is generally translated by the English pass., "to be added."

quis rebus = *quibus rebus*, abl. of means

sibi dat. of advantage

multos ex Romanis abl. with prep. instead of partitive gen.

familiari amicitia abl. governed by *coniunxerat*, "in a close friendship." In political contexts, *amicitia* describes the relationship between Rome and another state or individual; it was not formally ratified by treaty, but was an agreement of trust on which political alliances were built.

The African excursus, 17–19

According to Cicero in his rhetorical treatise *De Oratore*, the treatment of important and memorable achievements requires the historian to narrate not only the chronological order of events but also topographical descriptions (*regionum descriptionem*, 2.63). Ethnographic descriptions in Latin literature give us a glimpse of Roman cultural ethnocentricity, since the descriptions assume that Rome was the center of the known world; the location of the Italian peninsula in the Mediterranean lends credence to this belief (see also Claassen 1993). Ethnographic descriptions allow the orator or the historian to talk about the distinction between Roman and non-Roman in terms of "us and them." Romans also appear to have subscribed to the ancient Greek philosophical principle that climate affects character. The physical characteristics of a people derive from their physical environment, so that by describing the place of origin, the writer can at the same time establish character.

The custom of describing far-off places dates back to the sixth century and the Ionian historians; Herodotus wrote extensively about Egypt (*Histories* Book 2). The campaigns of Alexander the Great opened up new lands and peoples to the Greeks for the Hellenistic historians to describe. By Sallust's time, an ethnographic digression was expected to include information about physical geography, climate, crops, and raw material, as well as social and political institutions, religious customs, and military organization. Yet such information was provided not for study or instruction, but for entertainment and enjoyment. The reader should not expect carefully researched facts, but rather curious, mythical, and strange stories to engage the imagination (see Horsfall 1985).

Since Sallust was a governor of the province of Africa Nova, we can assume he had a certain amount of firsthand knowledge; and yet, he claims to be at the mercy of his sources (17.7). The description of Africa further develops the characterization of Jugurtha and reinforces the distinction between the Roman and non-Roman identities at war. In addition, Morstein-Marx suggests that the digression allows Sallust to evoke the Parthians, a formidable threat in Sallust's own day. The Romans had suffered a terrible defeat at Carrhae in 53, and unsuccessful campaigns waged between 41 and 36 failed to avenge the disaster. Thus, the drawn-out fighting with the Parthians casts a shadow across the *Bellum Iugurthinum* (2001, 192).

Wiedemann (1993) examines the three digressions in the *BI*; see also Green (1993); on the relationship between geography, ethnography, and the larger rubric of historiography, see Marincola (1999). For further reading on topographical digressions in general, see Thomas (1982) and Vasaly (1993, 131–55).

Sallust describes four main geographical features: the coastal lowlands, fertile but without suitable harbors; the maritime mountain ranges with deeply cut valleys supporting some agriculture; the high plateau or steppe, inhabited by nomads; and the southern Sahara ranges, hot and barren. The whole area, some 1,500 square miles, is characterized by a dominant complex of mountain ranges that run east-west. Although these mountains obstruct travel between the coast and the interior, they provide deep valleys for relatively unobstructed transport and communication along east-west routes.

17.1 **paucis** supply *uerbis*. This is the first of four references to brevity or quickness of composition in the excursus: *quam paucissumis*, 17.2 and 17.7; *tempus monet*, 19.2. Such repetition calls attention to the status of the excursus as a separate unit, less worthy of detail than the rest of the monograph. References to speed also allow Sallust to turn a liability into a virtue. He can give the impression that he is adept at handling his material; his account will be expedient, and therefore expert.

exponere et . . . adtingere supply the subject *me* for these infinitives governed by *postulare*, each preceded by its object (*situm* and *gentis*) in parallel word order.

nobis dat. of possession, i.e., the Romans

17.2 **item** adv. used as conj. in the prepositional phrase, "and likewise on account of"

narrauerim potential subjunctive

quam paucissumis *quam* + superl., *uerbis* is omitted for brevity

17.3   **Africam** The number of continents was disputed in antiquity and it was unclear whether Africa formed its own continent or was part of Europe.

  esse in indirect statement governed by *posuere*

17.4   **Ea** i.e., Africa

  finis acc. pl. in apposition to *fretum* and *latitudinem*, "as its borders"

  fretum nostri maris et Oceani the straits of Gibraltar; *nostri maris* = the Mediterranean, a patent expression of cultural ethnocentricity

  decliuem latitudinem hypallage, or interchange of adj. and noun, "broad sloping extent"

  Catabathmon a Greek acc., meaning "descent." This sandy plateau begins east of Cyrenaica on the north coast and gradually slopes towards the Nile valley; the area corresponds roughly to the dividing line between Egypt and modern Lybia (see map).

17.5   **Mare** supply *est*

  ager modified by three adjs. in chiasmus that contrasts positive and negative attributes

  frugum gen. pl. with *fertilis* denoting fullness

  pecori, arbori dats. of advantage and disadvantage

  caelo terraque abl. of cause, "because of the climate and the soil"

17.6   **salubri corpore** abl. of description

  laborum objective gen.

  nisi qui = *praeter eos qui*

  ferro aut bestiis abls. of means

  malefici generis "of a baneful kind"

17.7   In this lengthy periodic sentence, Sallust calls attention to his status as historian in the first person (*nobis, dicam*), signaling the excursus as a product of research (*ex libris Punicis*) and composition (*quam paucissumis*).

habuerint . . . adcesserint . . . permixti sint subjunctives in indirect question introduced by *qui . . . quique . . . aut quo modo*, governed by *dicam*

quamquam . . . diuorsum est, tamen . . . dicam Sallust concedes that his account will differ from general opinion.

quae plerosque obtinet "which prevails among many"

diuorsum nom. sing. n., predicate, the subject is the content of the three indirect questions

uti . . . utique These indicative clauses express the two authoritative sources on which Sallust relies: the books of King Hiempsal II (104–60, not to be confused with Hiempsal son of Micipsa murdered by Jugurtha in 116) translated from the Punic language, and the firsthand accounts of the inhabitants themselves. Although Greek was common throughout the Mediterranean, Punic was widely used in North Africa after the destruction of Carthage in 146. Because the royal family supported the literary arts, *regis Hiempsalis* may suggest that Hiempsal attempted to pass the books under his own name ("written by King Hiempsal"). It is more likely, however, that because Hiempsal inherited the library of the Carthaginian kings, the gen. simply denotes possession ("belonging to King Hiempsal"). See Matthews (1972).

interpretatum . . . est deponent used passively. On the translation of books from Punic to Latin, see Matthews (1972).

nobis dat. of reference, the pl. is common for Latin writers speaking of themselves, "translated for me" (not "by me," as abl. of agent requires a prep.). Sallust must rely not only on the books of Hiempsal but upon the accuracy of the translation. Matthews (1972) suggests that Sallust would have had recourse to these books during his governorship of Africa Nova in 46.

rem sese habere idiomatic, "the matter really is," cf. 85.23

quam paucissumis cf. *BI* 17.2

penes auctores Sallust abjures responsibility, which rests solely upon his sources, however unreliable they may be. The prep. *penes* almost always occurs with the verb *esse*.

18.1   **Africam initio habuere** echoes *initio Africam habuerint*, 17.7, a repetition that would seem to belie the claim of *quam paucissumis*, "as few words as possible"

quis = *quibus*, dat. of possession

caro ferina nom. sing. f., "game"

uti pecoribus refers only to *humi pabulum*

18.2   **quas** acc. pl. f., antecedent *sedes*

18.3   **Hercules** The Greek hero, whose twelve labors took him as far west as Geryon, ultimately died by burning on Mt. Oeta in central Greece. He is identified with Melcarth, a Phoenician hero. In Gades (modern Cadiz), an early Phoenician colony, there was a famous and wealthy sanctuary of Hercules/Melcarth. The African story, that Heracles died in Spain and his army scattered to Africa, suggests that the Hercules/Melcarth myth represents the spread of civilization through Phoenician commerce and colonization. But the Romans also claimed a part of Hercules' story. After Hercules destroyed the monster Cacus, King Evander established the Ara Maxima and Hercules himself performed the initial rites (*Aeneid* 8.184–279; Livy 1.7.3–15). The phrase *sicuti Afri putant* (i.e., as told in the books of Hiempsal) suggests that like the Romans, the Africans too told stories of a legendary past.

ex uariis gentibus abl. of source or material

ac conj. connecting the two abl. absolutes, *amisso duce* and *multis . . . petentibus*

quisque nom. sing.; techically the abl. pl. *quibusque* is required, but *sibi quisque* is a stock expression, "many, each for himself"

breui = *in breui tempore*

18.4   **Medi, Persae et Armenii** pl. denoting the peoples from the army of Hercules. Media, the country of the Medes, was situated in the mountainous region southwest of the Caspian Sea (modern Iran). It was eventually supplanted and absorbed by the Persian Empire. Armenia lay north of the Euphrates (see map). Located between the Roman and Parthian Empires, Armenia was regarded in Sallust's day as a strategic zone. The colonization of the western Mediterranean by these groups of people is not attested elsewhere.

nauibus abl. of means

nostro mari dat. governed by *proxumos*; another reminder of Roman ethnocentricity

18.5   **intra Oceanum magis** supply *manebant*, "they kept more toward the Ocean," i.e., nearer. In ancient thought, *Oceanus* was a vast river thought to surround the landmass formed by Europe, Asia, and Africa.

iique nom. pl. m., the Persians; *-que* connects two independent clauses, *intra Oceanum magis* (supply *manebant*) and *habuere = habuerunt*

pro tuguriis The makeshift huts, as opposed to grand architecture, give the impression of rustic and primitive people; the image idealizes simplicity as the opposite of civilization with its art and technology. Thus, Sallust implies a difference between the primitive Africans ("them") and the civilized Romans ("us").

emundi aut mutandi gen. gerunds depending on *copia*, "an opportunity for buying or bartering"

18.6   **ignara** used passively, "unknown"

conmercio abl. of separation with *prohibebant*

18.7   **Ii** i.e., the Persians

per conubia . . . miscuere Eventually nostalgic simplicity gives way to assimilation. By intermarriage, settlers and natives appear to dissolve their cultural differences under mutually agreeable conditions. For the Romans, the story of the Sabine women served a similar purpose (Livy 1.9–13).

et connects *miscuere = miscuerunt* and *appellauere = appellauerunt*, below

agros acc. pl. m., object of transitive pple. *temptantes*

alia, deinde alia loca acc. pl. n., "some places, then others"

petiuerant indicative in causal clause introduced by *quia*

semet enclitic *-met* for emphasis

18.8 **mapalia** a Punic word, almost always in the pl. as a collection of moveable huts, so that it comes to denote a way of life whereby the nomads as a group would pull up stakes and move to the next place. Judging from its use in Vergil *Geo.* 3.340, Lucan 4.684, and Tacitus, *Hist.* 4.50.4, *mapalia* are a commonly identified attribute of the Africans.

incuruis lateribus abl. of means

18.9 **Medis ... Armeniis** dat. with *adcessere* = *adcesserunt*, "settled next to"

propius compar. construed with acc., "more near the African sea," i.e., the western Mediterranean

agitabant supply *uitam*

sub sole magis i.e., further south; for the compar. with prepositional phrase, cf. 18.5, *intra Oceanum magis*

ab ardoribus "from the fierce heat of the torrid zone," i.e., "from the equator"

iique i.e., Medes, Armenians, and Lybians

freto abl. of means with *diuisi*, "separated by a narrow strait from Spain," cf. 18.5, *ab Hispanis*

18.10 **corrupere** = *corruperunt*

barbara lingua the etymology *Mauros pro Medis* is specious

18.11 **breui** = *in breui tempore*

nomine abl. sing. qualifying *Persarum*, "under the name of Numidians"

possedere = *possederunt*, the subject is *Persae* supplied from *Persarum*

proxuma superl. construed with acc., "nearest to Carthage," cf. the compar. + acc. *propius mare*, 18.9

appellatur attracted to the sing. *Numidia*, although the subject is the pl. *quae*

18.12   **freti** nom. pl. m., modifying *utrique*, "both," and governing the dat. *alteris*, "relying upon the other"

armis aut metu abls. of means

coegere . . . addidere = *coegerunt . . . addiderunt*

magis ii "especially those"

nostrum mare the third time the Mediterranean is so designated (*BI* 17.4, 18.4)

quia supply *erant* for the causal clause

quam with the compar. adv. *minus*; the two things compared (*Libyes* and *Gaetuli*) are in the same case (nom.)

Denique The adv. summarizes and brings this part of the history to a close.

Africae pars inferior pleraque "most of the lower part of Africa," i.e., the coastal lands near the Mediterranean which are lower in elevation

ab Numidis abl. of pers. agent

imperantium gen. pl. m., substantive pple., "of the rulers"

concessere = *concesserunt*

19.1   **alii . . . cupidine** *uariatio* in diction (*alii . . . pars*) and syntax (*gratia* + gerundive and abl. of cause) emphasizes the different motives for establishing colonies

domi locative

gratia governs *multitudinis minuendae*, gerundive expressing purpose

cupidine abl. of cause

et connects the two abl. absolutes, *sollicitata plebe* and *aliis . . . auidis* in which the motives for colonization are described using Roman political diction (*plebe* and *nouarum rerum*, cf. *BC* 28.4). Elsewhere in the monograph, Jugurtha's Numidians are described as "greedy for revolution" (*nouarum rerum auidum* 46.3) and "desirous of revolution" (*cupidum nouarum rerum*, 66.2).

Hipponem Hadrumetum Leptim asyndeton. Hippo Zarytus (not Hippo Regius, the city of Saint Augustine); Hadrumetum, a seaport 60 miles south of Carthage; Leptis Minor (not to be confused with Letpis Magna, further east, the site of exceptionally well-preserved ruins including a forum, theater, market, amphitheater, circus, and bath). See map.

condidere = *condiderunt*

multum adverbial acc.

pars . . . aliae *uariatio* in chiasmus with *alii . . . pars* above

praesidio . . . decori dats. of purpose in parallel word order with the noms. *pars . . . aliae*, sharing the same dat. of reference *originibus suis* ("their own mother cities"); for the double dat., see *BI* 6.2

19.2   **silere . . . dicere** The antonyms are epexegetical infinitives with *melius* (supply *esse*), "better to be silent than to say too little." Silence trumps *breuitas*. Sallust refrains from venturing into an account of Carthage; it is better for the sake of brevity to be silent than to risk speaking inadequately or without dignity. Sallust thus demonstrates an admiration for Rome's most formidable enemy. By declining to digress further, he reminds the reader that he is in the midst of a digression. Like *dicam* at 17.7, the statement calls attention to the historian's presence in the narrative (again with the first person, *puto*); however, in 17.7 Sallust put responsibility on his sources (*penes auctores*) while at 19.2, he expresses anxiety over his own possible shortcoming (*silere melius . . . quam parum dicere*) and the limitations imposed by *breuitas* (*tempus monet*). The two self-referential statements (17.7 and 19.2) frame the central panel of the excursus, paragraph 18: the origins and development of the peoples of Africa, from the beginning (*initio*, 18.1) to the rise of empire (*imperantium*, 18.12).

alio adv., "elsewhere"

properare tempus supply *me*, governed by *monet*. Sallust surely heeds time's warning: asyndeton (*Hipponem Hadrumetum*

Leptim), paratactic generalizing summary (*eaeque breui multum auctae*), and brachyology (application of *originibus* to two dats. of purpose) contribute to the *breuitas* of the excursus.

19.3   **Igitur** Sallustian word order

ad Catabathmon Starting at Catabathmos (already mentioned at 17.4), Sallust guides the reader on this tour of north Africa with step-by-step adverbial phrases: *secundo mari . . . deinceps. . . deinde . . . usque ad . . . super . . . post . . . dehinc.*

Aegyptum ab Africa It was disputed in antiquity whether Egypt was in the continent of Africa or Asia. Herodotus leaves it uncertain, but for Sallust (17.3–4), Egypt must be in Asia.

secundo mari abl. absolute, "with the sea following," "in the direction along the coast," i.e., westward from Catabathmos

Cyrene a major Greek colony founded from the island of Thera (modern Santorini, see map) in 630 that also gave its name to the surrounding territory of Cyrenaica; for the founding of the colony and its legendary King Battus, see Herodotus 4.150–58; for a later description of Cyrenaica, see Pliny the Elder *Natural History* 5.31. The temple of Battus is mentioned in Catullus 7.6.

Theraeon Greek gen. pl., cf. *Philaenon* below

duae Syrtes notoriously dangerous shallows off the Lybian coast of north Africa from Cyrenaica to Tunisia. The Lesser Syrtis is known today as the Gulf of Cabès and the Greater Syrtis as the Gulf of Sydra; between them lies Sabrata, Leptis, and Oea, three cities (modern Tripoli) that prospered in spite of the navigational dangers posed by the Syrtes. Pliny the Elder describes the Syrtes in detail (*Natural History* 5.25–26).

Philaenon arae *Philaenon*, Greek gen. pl. The Philaeni were two Carthaginian brothers who agreed to be buried alive to establish the frontier between their country and Cyrene; *Philaenon arae* is a settlement commemorating the spot (see map). While Sallust conspicuously stops himself from a digression on Carthage, he goes on to recount in detail the fascinating story of the brothers at *BI* 79 (not in this volume's selections). The brothers' self-sacrifice contrasts pointedly with the fratricide of Romulus and Remus and with Jugurtha's premeditated murder of his adoptive brothers; Hiempsal was betrayed and hunted down (*BI* 12), Adherbal was tortured and slaughtered (*BI* 26).

uorsus anastrophe of prep. and acc. object

habuere = *habuerunt*

19.4 **proxumi Hispanias** superl. construed with acc., "nearest to Spain," cf. *proxuma* at *BI* 18.11. *Hispianias* is pl. because Spain was formally constituted as two separate coastal provinces, *Hispania Citerior* and *Hispania Ulterior* in 197. Both were extended inland until most of the peninsula was in Roman hands by 133.

19.5 **accepimus** Sallust signals his source; whether derived from the books of King Hiempsal or some other geographer, this knowledge is secondhand.

partim . . . alios the third such variation in the paragraph, with etymologizing stem repetition in the adv. *partim* for calculated imbalance

incultius compar. adv., *uariatio* with the prepositional phrase *in tuguriis*

agitare . . . esse infinitives in indirect statement governed by *accepimus*; with *agitare* supply *uitam*, cf. *BI* 18.9

19.6 **Aethiopas** Greek acc. pl. m. Ethiopia was the name used by the Greeks for any region in the far south, and eventually for the lands south of Egypt; the etymology suggests the land of the "Burnt Faced" people.

ardoribus abl. of means

19.7 **bello Iugurthino** for the abl. of time, cf. *BI* 7.2, *bello Numantino*

pleraque ex Punicis abl. with prep. instead of partitive gen.

nouissume superl. adv., "most recently," i.e., between the end of the second and end of the third Punic wars, 201–146. The tax-paying province of Africa was formed after the destruction of Carthage in 146. Although Sallust refrains from the indigenous history and ethnography of Carthage, he clearly and succinctly states its provincial status.

habuerant supply the subject from *Carthaginiensium*

per magistratus Traditionally assigned by the Senate, posts in the provinces were filled by consuls or praetors, who governed after they had completed their term of office at Rome. Decisions about provincial posts were usually made immediately after the magistrates took up office on the Ides of March.

flumen Muluccham separated the kingdoms of Bocchus and Jugurtha, whose treasury was located at a fort on the river which Marius was able to capture; see *BI* 92.5–94

sub Iugurtha With the prepositional phrase, Sallust starts to steer the digression back onto course (the war with Jugurtha).

Mauris omnibus dat. governed by *imperitabat*

rex Bocchus This is the first mention of Bocchus, who eventually plays a pivotal role in the war. Jugurtha married his daughter; for the Romans, such marriages strengthened political alliances; however, because the Numidians were polygamous, such alliances carried less weight (*BI* 80.3–7). Jugurtha tried to manipulate Bocchus, but eventually Sulla was able to induce the king to betray Jugurtha to the Romans.

praeter nomen i.e., the name of Rome was universally known

cetera adverbial acc., "as to everything else"

populi Romani objective gen. with *ignarus*, "unaware of the Roman people"

itemque connects the two adjs. *ignarus* and *cognitus* modifying *rex Bocchus*

nobis dat. with *cognitus*

neque bello neque pace abls. of time, measured in starkly imperialistic terms, characterizing Bocchus as neither enemy nor friend

cognitus etymologizing stem repetition with *ignarus* for an agreeable and euphonious close to the periodic sentence

19.8   **ad necessitudinem rei** expressing purpose, "to meet the needs of the matter"

satis dictum supply *est*. Sallust uses the same phrase to close his account of the so-called first Catilinarian conspiracy (not in this volume's selections, *BC* 19.6): *de superiore coniuratione satis dictum*, "about the earlier conspiracy enough has been said." The tone of finality and closure in the phrase *satis dictum* is imposing, yet contrived, since Sallust admitted earlier that he left out important information about Carthage because of time constraints, and later in the monograph he will tell the story of the Philaeni brothers (*BI* 79). Thus, throughout the digression, both Sallust and his reader are acutely aware of the larger narrative that demands full attention.

Marius prepares for campaign, 84

Returning to the war with Jugurtha, Sallust narrates events from the division of Numdia to the outbreak of the war (chapters 20–28). After the murder of Hiempsal and the defeat and death of Adherbal, Rome declared war on Jugurtha in 112. Calpurnius Bestia commanded the army in Numidia and began a vigorous campaign. But Jugurtha tempted Bestia with bribery. He came into the Roman camp and conducted secret negotiations with Bestia; he handed over elephants, cattle, horses, and silver in exchange for peace. When news of this reached Rome, there was public outcry. Meanwhile, Bestia's men committed further outrages: some sold back the elephants for a profit, others sold deserters, all looted indiscriminately. Jugurtha was summoned to Rome to give evidence about these disgraceful acts, but the tribune's veto prevented him from speaking, and so Bestia and his men went unpunished. Jugurtha returned to Numidia.

The next year (111), Spurius Albinus was consul and given command of Roman forces, but he too was unsuccessful. The Romans suspected him of complicity because he did not finish the war; Albinus returned to Rome leaving his brother Aulus in command. Jugurtha took advantage of Aulus' inexperience and incompetence (chapters 29–40).

The shameful humiliation caused by Bestia and Albinus prompts Sallust to digress on party politics at Rome in chapters 41–42 before narrating the campaigns of Quintus Metellus (chapters 43–83). He campaigned for two years, but he was unable to defeat Jugurtha. In 108, one of Metellus' deputies, Marius, was elected consul for 107 and was appointed to replace him. The appointment was made by the popular assembly, which overrode the Senate. Granting all of Marius' requests for supplies and reinforcements, the Senate mistakenly believed that his popularity would be short lived and that the citizenry did not really support his efforts; however, the people were eager to enlist because of the promise of otherwise unattainable financial profit. Marius, using class prejudice to his advantage, inveighed against the nobility. See von Fritz (1943).

84.1-2   **At Marius . . . proficisci** Marius is the subject of this periodic sentence that begins with a circumstantial pple. and an adj. (*factus* and *infestus*), followed by eight historical infinitives: *instare, laedere, dictitare, habere, postulare, arcessere, adcire,* and *cogere*. The first three infinitives describe Marius' insults and boasts; *prima habere* moves to Marius' reasoning; the last four infinitives express his increasing activity and aggression in preparing for the campaign.

84.1   **ut supra diximus** for the pl., see 17.7 (*nobis*); anticipates *cupientissuma plebe*, explained at 73.6–7 (not in this volume's selections): "Finally, the common people were so inflamed that all craftsmen and field workers, whose means and livelihoods rested in their own hands, left their work and crowded around Marius and ranked their own needs second to his honor. So after many storms the consulship was bestowed upon a new man, while the nobility was stunned" (*BI* 73.6–7). Thus the content of 73.6–7 is reduced to an abl. absolute for *breuitas*; rather than repeat information, Sallust makes the reader responsible for information contained in the cross reference. Sallust uses this sort of directional signal less often in the *Bellum Iugurthinum* than in the *Bellum Catilinae*.

cupientissuma plebe abl. absolute without a pple. (Latin lacks the pres. pple. of *esse*), "because of the very eagerly desiring plebs"

ei dat. with *iussit*

prouinciam Numidiam Technically, Numidia did not have provincial status until 193 CE; *prouinciam* simply means "sphere of influence" or "proconsular sphere of activity," also explained by the cross reference to 73.7: "When the people were asked by the tribune of the plebs Titus Manlius Mancinus whom they wished to wage war with Jugurtha, they bid for Marius in unison. But a little before, the Senate had decreed Numidia to Metellus; that matter was in vain" (*BI* 73.7).

nobilitati dat. with *infestus*; for the semantics of *nobilitas*, cf. *BC* 23.6

multus atque ferox nom. adjs. in Latin are elegantly rendered by English advs., "often and fiercely"

singulos modo, modo uniuorsos chiasmus

illis abl. pl. m., antecedent *nobilitati*, a collective sing. rendered pl.

spolia n. pl., in apposition to *consulatum*, "as booty," as Comber and Balmaceda note, the metaphor derives from the custom of stripping a slain enemy of his armor, thus making the consulship a matter not of internal politics among citizens but of external warfare among enemies

alia acc. pl. n., object of *dictitare*, modified by antithetical adjs. in chiasmus: *magnifica pro se*, "splendid on behalf of himself" and *et illis dolentia*, "and annoying to them"

illis dat. with *dolentia*

84.2   **quae bello opus erant** *quae*, nom. pl. n., subject of *erant*; *bello* dat. of purpose; *opus* predicate nom., "what things were essential for the war"

legionibus dat. of advantage; legionaries were recruited from Roman citizens

auxilia a populis et regibus auxiliary forces from independent states and monarchies, allies of Rome outside of Italy

ex Latio sociisque Latin and Italian allies. After Rome's conquest of Italy, communities in the peninsula were obliged to equip and furnish troops attached to the consular army. The pressure of this military service was one of the causes of the Social Wars of 90–89. Marius uses every possible resource: citizen legionaries, auxiliaries from outside Italy, and allies from the peninsula. As he raises troops fom the Latin and Italian allies to supplant Metellus, so Sulla will in turn raise troops from the same reserve to supplant Marius: "Lucius Sulla the quaestor arrived with a host of cavalry in camp, which he had been left at Rome to muster from Latium and from the allies" (*BI* 95.1).

fortissumum quemque "each of the bravest" (cf. *BC* 61.7 for *quisque* + superl.)

plerosque . . . paucos . . . cognitos in apposition to *fortissumum quemque*, "the majority known in the field (i.e., by fighting with him before), a few by reputation (only)"

militiae locative "in the field," "in war," usually with *domi*; cf. *BC* 29.3

fama abl. of cause

et connecting *adcire* and *cogere*

ambiundo gerund, abl. of means

emeritis stipendiis abl. of description with *homines*, "men with earned pay," i.e., retired veterans

proficisci infinitive governed by *cogere*

84.3   **illi** dat. indirect object governed by *abnuere*

laetus "gladly"

neque plebi militia uolenti putabatur supply *esse*, *militia* is nom. subject of *neque putabatur*, the pple. *uolenti* modifies the dat. *plebi*, "military service was not thought to be to the people as wishing it," i.e., "military service was not thought to be to the liking of the people." This is a Greek construction found in Thucydides and first used in Latin by Sallust. The use of such a native Greek idiom suggests a degree of foreignness; good Romans should be willing to serve in the army.

belli usum "the need of war," i.e., men required for the campaign; note the chiasmus with *studia uolgi*

cum Mario abl. of accompaniment

eundi gerund objective gen.

84.4 **praeda** abl. with *locupletem*, "rich in booty"

domum acc. of motion toward

rediturum conditional pple., "should he return a victor"

alia huiusce modi cf. *BC* 15.1

animis trahebant idiomatic, "each was occupied with the thought," "was imagining," governs *fore*, *rediturum* (supply *esse*), and *alia*, the subject is the singular *quisque*

non paulum litotes

oratione sua abl. of means. All Roman statesmen needed to be skilled public speakers to achieve their political aims.

84.5 **omnibus ... decretis** abl. absolute

hortandi ... exagitandi gens. of gerund with *causa*, connected by *simul et*, "and at the same time"

nobilitatem acc. object of *exagitandi*

contionem populi The *contio* was a public meeting called by an elected magistrate to inform the people of matters of general public interest and welfare. The speaker stood at the *rostra*, a platform close to the senate house that was adorned with the beaks (*rostra*) of captured ships. Sallust probably delivered a *contio* when he served as tribune. See Taylor (1966, especially chapter 2) for the different types of *contiones*; Morstein-Marx (2004) for the purpose and audience; Tan (2008) for the composition of the audience.

hoc modo abl. of manner; for the disclaimer (repeated at 86.1), see Introduction, xxxi–xxxii

The speech of Marius, 85

Marius asks the people to decide who has the moral high ground, himself or the nobility. He is defensive about his status as a *nouus homo* and derisive of the nobility. He asks the audience whether they regret having elected him consul. But in the end, his purpose is clearly stated: he seeks men to enlist in his army.

As with all speeches in ancient historiography, this is not a faithful transcript but approximates what the speaker is likely to have said, so as to convey not only the speaker's intentions, but also the historian's themes and attitudes (on speech in Latin historiography, see Miller 1975). As Sklenár notes, "One of the most arresting features of Sallust's historiographical procedure is his tendency in speeches to retain the unique characteristics of his own language rather than to duplicate that of the speakers themselves. The effect . . . is to make the speaker sound like the historian" (1998, 205). Indeed, several turns of phrase in Marius' speech are also found in this volume's other selections.

According to ancient rhetorical theory, there are three types of speeches: forensic speeches delivered in law courts, deliberative speeches delivered before decision-making bodies, such as the Senate, and epideictic or display speeches delivered before a public assembly. In an epideictic speech, the orator usually praises his city; for example, he may deliver a eulogy for soldiers fallen in battle. Since Marius' speech is addressed to citizens and delivered at a *contio* or public assembly, it is technically epideictic; however, it is hardly a panegyric of Rome. Instead it is a scathing prosecution of the nobility. Furthermore, because he asks the people to reaffirm their decision to elect him, the speech is also deliberative. So as Marius shifts register from forensic to deliberative to epideictic, he adopts an appropriate Greek model; he quotes from a forensic speech of Lysias, a deliberative speech of Demosthenes, and epideictic speeches of Isocrates and Plato.

The speech falls into four parts, the *exordium* (introduction, 85.1–9), *confirmatio* (argumentation, 85.10–25), *refutatio* (anticipation of opponent's arguments, 85.26–43), and *peroratio* (summary and closing, 85.44–50). In the *exordium*, the speaker must gain his audience's attention and goodwill. Although the opening gambit is somewhat general, by beginning with disparaging remarks, Marius takes a calculated risk and assumes that his audience shares his disdain for the nobility. He begins by drawing a contrast between himself and the nobility, hence the paragraph is rife with the comparative degree and antithetical pronouns.

85.1   **Quirites** The standard way for an orator to address the citizens of Rome at the beginning of a *contio*; cf. Cicero *In Catilinam* 2.1 and 3.1. According to Livy, when the Romans struck a truce with the Sabines (thanks to the intervention of the Sabine women), they shared authority but transferred the seat of governance to Rome. In order to grant some concession to the Sabines, the citizens were named *Quirites*, from the town of Cures (Livy 1.13.4–5). The term refers to citizens specifically in their civil, peacetime functions. Marius calls upon them to set aside this name and become soldiers in his army.

non isdem artibus abl. of means, "not with the same practices"

imperium acc. object of both *petere* and *gerere*, infinitives in indirect statement governed by *Scio*

primo "at first," i.e., when seeking office

industrios supplicis modicos asyndeton, *supplicis* = *supplices*

dein corresponds to *primo*, "then," i.e., when performing the duties of office

mihi dat. of person regularly used after *uidetur*, "it seems to me"

contra ea supply *esse*; predicate prepositional phrase as adj., "otherwise"

85.2   **quo . . . eo** abls. of degree of difference, "the more . . . the greater"

pluris gen. of indef. value, "by how much the entire is of greater value than the consulship or the praetorship"

quam with compar. *pluris*; the two things compared (*res publica* and *consulatus aut praetura*) are in the same case (nom.)

maiore cura abl. of manner, "with care (all) the greater," compar. with *quam*; the two things compared are syntactically equivalent: *illam administrari debere* and *haec peti debere*

illam . . . haec "the former . . . the latter," i.e., *res publica* and *consulatus aut praetura*; *haec* is acc. n. pl.

debere governed by *uidetur*

85.3   **me** acc. after impers. *fallit*; the subject of *fallit* is the clause *quantum . . . sustineam*

beneficio i.e., the consulship. In Roman thought, *beneficium* or benefit was the chief bond of human society; it consisted not necessarily in the thing bestowed but in the wish to do good. Ingratitude for a *beneficium* was considered a grave wrong, so Marius is grateful for the kindness of the voters which he will repay by his conduct in office.

negoti partitive gen. with *quantum*, "how much business"

sustineam subjunctive in indirect question introduced by *quantum*

parare . . . et . . . parcere, cogere . . . , curare et . . . agere five infinitives arranged as a tricolon, the first and third in pairs joined by *et* and preceded by their objects, the middle a single infinitive followed by its object

nolis potential subjunctive in rel. clause introduced by *quos*, "whom you would not wish to offend." Occasionally in the speech, Marius uses the second person sing. so as to seem to address individual members of the audience.

domi forisque locative, "at home and abroad"

inuidos occursantis factiosos asyndeton, again the middle element with the alternate acc. pl. m. ending; cf. *industrios supplicis modicos*, 85.1

opinione abl. of comparison with *asperius*, "than belief," "than you (*Quirites*) would imagine"

est sing. implies that any one of the subject infinitives would be more difficult than belief

85.4   **alii** hyperbaton for emphasis

deliquere = *deliquerunt*, indicative in a general condition introduced by *si*

uetus . . . clientelae chiasmus of adjs. and gens. before the nouns, the central elements in subtle *uariatio. Clientelae* were distinctive dependents, whole communities either in Italy or in the provinces who sought the protection and influence of Roman leaders. The *nobilitas* would have gained *clientelae* by their deeds (*facta*) and by their means (*opes*).

maiorum fortia facta Especially attentive to precedent and tradition, the Romans venerated their elders (the oldest living senators).

omnia haec summarizes the four subjects of *adsunt*, i.e., all of the trappings of the nobility

praesidio dat. of purpose

mihi contrasts with *alii* for antithesis

memet enclitic -*met* for emphasis

sitae supply *sunt*

uirtute et innocentia abls. of means; note the alliteration with *tutari*. Albinus lacked military prowess, and Bestia was not above reproach, yet their noble lineage protected them. Marius, on the other hand, must be courageous and blameless. A similar sentiment is expressed in Lysias 14, the forensic prosecution of the son of Alcibiades for dereliction of duty: "So is it not terrible, men of the jury, that my opponents are so fortunate that when they are caught having committed crimes, they find haven because of their family, but we, if we suffer misfortune because of those who are reckless, are not able to register a plea?" (Lysias 14.18).

85.5 **conuorsa esse . . . fauere . . . quaerere** triad of infinitives in indirect discourse governed by *intellego*

aequos bonosque acc. subjects of *fauere*, supply *mihi* as dat. object

quippe introduces a parenthetical statement within the indirect discourse. The particle carries a sense of sarcasm or irony; it is the root of our English word "quip." Three times in the speech *quippe* introduces biting wit, "Well of course, *my* deeds well done benefit the Republic"

mea bene facta "my deeds well done" in return for *uostro beneficio* of the people, 85.3; etymologizing stem repetition + possessive adjs. emphasize the antithesis

rei publicae dat. with *procedunt*, "benefit the Republic"

locum inuadundi supply *me* for the objective gen. transitive gerund expressing purpose, "an opportunity for attacking (me)," "room to attack me"

85.6   **Quo** connecting rel. pron. = *et eo*, abl. of degree of difference with *acrius*

mihi dat. of agent with pass. periphrastic

capiamini . . . sint subjunctives in purpose clause introduced by *uti = ut*

neque . . . et coordinating the two subjunctives; *neque* negates *capiamini*, with a sense of being taken in or trapped, "both that you are not captured and that . . ."

illi nom., pl., m., i.e., the nobility, contrasts with *uos*

frustra predicate adv.; cf. *BI* 7.6 (also in penultimate position)

85.7   **aetatis** partitive gen. with *hoc*, "up to this time of life"

fui "I have lived"

consueta habeam pple. + subjunctive in a result clause introduced by *uti* and anticipated by *ita*, "so as to consider familiar," "so as to be accustomed to." The idiom *habere* + pple. indicates that the direct object has been brought into a certain condition by the action of the subject.

ante uostra beneficia "before your benefits," i.e., "before the kindness of your votes"

85.8   **ea** acc. pl. n., object of *deseram* in hyperbaton, antecedent of *quae*

accepta mercede abl. absolute, implying the consulship and making explicit the metaphor of commerce suggested by *pluris* (gen. of value) 85.2, *negotii* 85.3, *aerario* 85.3, and *procedunt* 85.5. Given the Romans' pejorative social attitudes towards commerce, trade, and money making, this sort of language can arouse resentment across a broad spectrum of citizens, both those who seek to better themselves through commerce and those who disdain it, clinging to the very attitudes that perpetuate economic inequality.

deseram subjunctive in substantive purpose clause introduced by *uti* and governed by *non est consilium*; at *BC* 4.1, the expression governs infinitives

85.9   **Illis** dat. with *difficile*, in clear contrast to *mihi* for antithesis

in potestatibus a somewhat exaggerated expression giving an unfavorable impression of how the nobility behaves when "in power," i.e., when in office

per ambitionem "while canvassing," i.e., while campaigning for office

simulauere = *simulauerunt*

in optumis artibus cf. *isdem artibus*, 85.1

bene facere infinitive, "to do well," i.e., to serve the state, subject of *uortit*. The infinitive as subject is not common except with *est* and similar verbs.

iam emphasizes Marius' innate nature, capable of change; by implication the nobility is static

85.10–25 The *confirmatio* is the main body of the speech, containing logical arguments as proof; the speaker appeals to reason. So having made his position clear, Marius next asks his audience to consider the consequences of their decision (already made) with four imperatives: *reputate* (85.10), *conparate* (85.13), *existumate* (85.14), and *uidete* (85.25). He asks them to weigh the decision based on a comparison of himself with the nobility, hence the continued preponderance of comparatives (*melius, pluris, clariores, praeclarior, flagitiosior, praeclarius*).

85.10   **Quaeso** softens the imperative, "I ask you," "please"

sit subjunctive in indirect question introduced by *num* and governed by *reputate*

quem for *aliquem*

globo the word carries a disparaging tone

mittatis subjunctive in the protasis of fut. less vivid condition introduced by *si*; the clause explains the content of the indirect question *num . . . melius sit*, "whether it would be better, if you should send"

hominem in apposition to *quem* above

ueteris prosapiae ac multarum imaginum et nullius stipendi parallel word order (adj./noun) in a tricolon of gens. of quality with *uariatio* of conjs., the middle, plural term flanked by singulars. *Prosapiae* is an archaic term used by Cato the Censor. *Imagines* are the ancestral face masks cast in wax that were kept in the atrium of the home and brought out for funerals (see Flower 1996, especially 16–31), when they were worn by individuals to impersonate the ancestors so as to raise the family to a noble status (see *BC* 23.6). At *BI* 4.5–6, Sallust privileges history above *imagines*: "For I have often heard that Quintus Maximus and Publius Scipio and other outstanding statesmen used to say that when they beheld the funeral masks of their ancestors, their courage was most powerfully roused to prowess. Yet it is not the wax nor the sculpting that has power in it, but the recording of history causes that flame to grow in the hearts of exceptional men" (*BI* 4.5–6). Yet Marius mentions *imagines* five times in this speech (85.10, 25, 29, 30, 38). *Stipendium* (especially when modified by an adj. of quantity) by metonymy means "military service." The polysyndeton contrasts the plentitude of the first two elements with the utter lack of the third, "no military service (whatsoever)"

scilicet ut . . . ignarus ironic, "as being someone ignorant"

omnium objective gen. with *ignarus* as at *BI* 19.7

trepidet, festinet, sumat pres. subjunctives in result clause, asyndeton suggests haste

85.11   **quem . . . is sibi** The emphatic, almost needless repetition of prons. is sarcastic; *sibi*, dat. of advantage

imperatorem noun agent derived from *imperare*

quaerat subjunctive, introduced by *ut* and governed by *euenit*

85.12   **Atque ego scio, Quirites** echoes first words of the speech

qui . . . coeperint rel. clause of characteristic. The initial position of *postquam consules facti sunt* within the rel. clause mocks the etymology of *praeposteri*, a compound adj. from *prae* ("before," also present in the word *praecepta*) + *post* ("after"), adding to the disparaging tone

et acta maiorum et Graecorum militaria praecepta chiasmus, "both the achievements of our ancestors and the military handbooks of the Greeks." Marius prefers Roman practice to Greek theory, deed to word. On *maiores*, see above, 85.4.

praeposteri homines in apposition to the rel. clause of characteristic, with etymological chiasmus of *postquam* and *praecepta*

nam . . . est Compression occludes the syntax but not the meaning of this *nam* clause that explains the *postquam consules facti sunt* clause. So, for *gerere*, supply *consulatum*; *fieri* is the infinitive of *facti sunt*, "For to conduct (the consulship) is later in time than to be elected, but in importance and experience it is earlier." On Sallust's expert use of *nam* clauses, see Frazer (1961). The sentence is practically a translation of the deliberative speech of Demosthenes, *Olynthiac* 3.15: "For in order of time, action is after speaking and voting, but in importance it is first and of more importance."

quam with compar. *posterius*; the two things compared are syntactically equivalent: *gerere quam fieri*

tempore posterius pleonastic abl. of time, again the reversed order of *posterius* (later) and *prius* (earlier) mocks the *praeposteri* for putting the cart before the horse

re atque usu abls. of specification, "in importance and experience"

85.13 **cum illorum superbia** the strained comparison of the concrete *me hominem nouom* with the abstract *superbia* allows Marius to scorn the nobility without pointing to individuals by name

hominem nouom in apposition to *me*; for the term, see *BC* 23.6

eorum partitive gen. with *partem* for *uariatio* with *alia*

egomet enclitic -*met* for emphasis

quae illi litteris supply the gapped *didicerunt* (brachyology)

litteris ... militando abls. of means

85.14 **pluris** cf. 85.2

sint subjunctive in indirect question introduced by *an*

mihi fortuna, illis probra parallel word order. Fortune not only means chance and luck, but it comes to develop the sense of rank, station, and wealth.

85.15 **Quamquam** in a corrective sense, "and yet," rarely used with independent clauses, imposes upon *sed* a sense of *tamen*

fortissumum quemque supply *esse*; for *quisque* + superl., cf. *BC* 61.7, *BI* 84.2

85.16 **ac si ... uoluisse?** an indirect or embedded prosopopoeia, a device by which an imaginary, absent, or dead person is represented as speaking or acting. Marius supposes a conversation between himself and the fathers of Albinus and Bestia, as if to call witnesses and in anticipation of the *refutatio*, or arguments of his opponents.

iam emphasizes the pres. contrary to fact condition, "if it were possible now"

Albini aut Bestiae see the introductory note to 84 for the blunders of these two generals

posset subjunctive in pres. contrary to fact condition introduced by *si*

mene the enclitic -*ne* introduces the first member of the alternative question

maluerint subjunctive in indirect alternative question introduced by *mene an*

sese . . . uoluisse indirect statement governed by *responsuros* (supply *fuisse*)

liberos quam optumos "the best children possible"

85.17 **faciant** hortatory subjunctive

maioribus suis dat. indirect object, "to their own ancestors"

uti = *ut* "as"

85.18 **honori . . . labori, innocentiae, periculis** dats. with *inuident . . . inuideant*. The shift from indicative to subjunctive lends authority to the demand; since the nobility (in fact) envy his office, then they should (in theory) also envy his risks.

per haec illum *haec*, acc. pl. n., antecedent *labori innocentiae periculis*; *illum*, acc. sing. m., antecedent *honori*, "by the latter I obtained the former"

85.19 **superbia** abl. of means with *corrupti*, echoes *cum illorum superbia*, 85.13

contemnant . . . uixerint subjunctives in conditional clauses of comparison introduced by *quasi* which implies the omitted apodoses, "as if they scorned . . . as if they had lived (but in fact they did not)"

honeste The adv. should not be confused with the English derivative, "honestly"; rather, in Latin it is always related to honor and means "honorably." The adj. *honesti* occurs at 85.49; it is echoed at 86.3 (*honesta*), in Sallust's description of the kinds of men who enlisted in Marius' army.

85.20 **Ne** The particle, cognate with the Greek νή or ναί, is almost always followed by the pers. pron. *ille* or *iste*. The expression must surely be ironic, given Marius' self-proclaimed disdain toward anything Greek.

ignauiae uoluptatem et praemia uirtutis in apposition to *res*; the chiasmus emphasizes the antithesis and depicts the broad distance denoted by the superl. adj. *diuorsissumas*

85.21   **quom . . . faciunt** *quom* + indicative for an iterative temporal clause, "whenever." For the ideological import of such iterative temporal clauses in the *BI*, see Fields 2007.

      pleraque oratione abl. of instrument, "in the greater part of their speech"

      eorum i.e., of their ancestors

      memorando transitive gerund, abl. of means

      clariores sese supply *esse* for indirect statement after *putant*

85.22   **contra** prep. as predicate adv., here colloquial; cf. *post* at *BC* 23.6

      quanto . . . tanto abls. of degree of difference

      uita supply *est*

      illorum . . . horum "of the former . . . of the latter"

85.23   **Et profecto ita se res habet** emphatically contrasts with *Quod contra est*, as if to say, "This is how it really is," for the idiom, cf. *BI* 17.7

      posteris dat. of advantage

      neque bona neque mala acc. pl. n., "it (glory) allows neither good nor bad deeds of them to be hidden"

      in occulto supply *esse*; predicate prepositional phrase as adj., "hidden," cf. *cum telo* at *BC* 27.2

85.24   **Huiusce rei** i.e., *maiorum gloria*; Marius lacks the glory of his ancestors

      fateor conveys sincerity that distances Marius from the heavy-handed irony and sarcasm deployed so far

      uerum conj., "but"

      id quod the clause in apposition to the *licet* clause

      multo abl. of degree of difference

      mihi dat. with impers. *licet*

85.25   **sint** subjunctive in indirect question introduced by *quam*

      quod . . . id "that which they claim for themselves (i.e., the consulship) . . . they do not yield"

      sibi dat. with *adrogant*

mihi dat. with *concedunt*

ex mea supply *uirtute*, "relying on others' excellence . . . relying on my own (excellence)." Note the chiasmus of dats. and prepositional phrases: *ex aliena uirtute sibi . . . mihi ex mea*

scilicet Marius returns to irony as he continues to belittle the importance of *imagines* to the nobility with two causal (*quia*) clauses. *Noua nobilitas* is an oxymoron, since true nobility is primordial, not freshly created.

mihi dat. of possession

quam acc. sing. f. rel. pron., antecedent *nobilitatem*, "which it is better to have gotten indisputably than to have corrupted once received"

quam with compar. *melius*; *peperisse* and *corrupisse* are syntactically equivalent epexegetical infinitives, but *certe* and *acceptam* lend variation

acceptam circumstantial pple. modifying *nobilitatem*, "once received"

85.26–43 In the *refutatio*, a speaker answers the counterarguments of his opponents. In contrast to the complicated comparative mode of the speech so far, Marius' style becomes much more lucid as he anticipates the claims of his opponents, who will use fancy language. He, on the other hand, speaks plainly.

85.26 **uelint** subjunctive in protasis of fut. less vivid condition introduced by *si*; the apodosis is the indirect statement *orationem fore*

illis dat. of possession with *fore*

fore a true fut. infinitive

in maxumo uostro beneficio see 85.3. The bulk of the speech pits Marius against the *nobilitas* using the compar. degree, but the superl. is reserved for public office; cf. below, *summum honorem et maxumum negotium*, 85.28

meque uosque verbose pleonasm contrasts with Sallust's usual *breuitas*

lacerent subjunctive in concessive clause introduced by *quom*

quis for *aliquis*

duceret subjunctive in negative purpose clause introduce by
ne, "lest anyone turn my reticence into guilt." Plain phrases
and simple verbs are the hallmark of Sallust's style; here, *ducere*
hovers between a concrete sense of "lead into" and an abstract
sense of "consider." The English idiom "turn into" retains the
sense of motion with the metaphor of mental activity.

85.27   **ex animi mei sententia** a formula in oaths, "in all honesty,"
"sincerely," undercut by the sarcastic tone of *quippe* that col-
ors the next clause.

uera . . . praedicent nom. pl. n. substantive subject of *praedicent*, subjunctive governed by *necesse est* without *ut*, "it is
necessary that truths proclaim well"

falsa . . . superant acc. pl. n. substantive as object of *superant*,
"the manner of my life prevails over falsehoods." The asyndeton of the two clauses (*necesse est* and *superunt*) emphasizes
the antithesis of *uera* and *falsa*, words with identical morphology but different syntax.

uita moresque hendiadys (use of two nouns with a conj., instead of single modified noun)

85.28   **mihi** dat. with *inposuistis*, second person pl. after *uostra*

eorum gen. of the cause of feeling with impers. pass. periphrastic *paenitendum sit*, "whether it is necessary that you be regret-
ful of these (measures)," "whether you must regret them"

sit subjunctive in indirect question introduced by *num*

85.29   **causa** anastrophe

postulet subjunctive in protasis of fut. less vivid condition introduced by *si*

hastas, uexillum, phaleras asyndeton for cumulative effect,
the middle singular term flanked by plurals. The *hasta do-
natica* was a headless spear awarded for valor; the *uexillum*
a replica of a military banner awarded for distinguished service; *phalerae* were medals worn on the breastplate.

alia militaria dona Elsewhere as the fourth element after a tricolon, *alia* is rather hollow (e.g., *BC* 15.1), but here it summarizes the list and impresses upon the audience the hardships Marius has endured.

aduorso corpore abl. absolute. The nobility has only malleable waxen images of others; Marius has indelible scars of his own. By mentioning scars, Marius exceeds the bounds of decorum to prove his extraordinary valor (*uirtus*); his scars prove that he faced the enemy. In the absence of *imagines*, Marius must rely on military achievement and the testimony of his scars. War wounds properly incurred, i.e., facing the enemy (cf. *BC* 61.3), are often displayed as evidence of character, service, or trustworthiness; on the rhetoric of wounds, see Leigh (1995).

85.30   **hae . . . haec** anaphora for emphasis

hereditate abl. of means

relicta . . . illa . . . quae nom. pl. n., referring to both *imagines* and *nobilitas*

illis dat. of reference

plurumis laboribus et periculis echoes 85.18; the superl. and the pls. contrast with the sing. *hereditate*

85.31   **Non sunt conposita uerba mea** Perhaps the most ironic statement of the speech, for clearly each word is carefully calculated and masterfully arranged. The disclaimer lets Marius imply that his opponents are sly, deceitful, cunning, and thereby untrustworthy, without saying as much. Normally such implications are made using *praeteritio* (the act of drawing attention to something by professing to omit it, e.g., "I will not mention his cunning"), however *praeteritio* detracts from *breuitas*. Instead, the utter silence allows Marius to condemn his opponents the more soundly and align himself with the common people.

parui gen. of value, idiomatic with *id facio*, "I regard it of little value"

satis Although Marius' language is a bit too clipped and his opponents' a bit too excessive, *uirtus* knows just how much to reveal herself.

illis artificio dat. of reference, abl. of thing needed, idiomatic with *opus est*, "they need contrivance"

tegant subjunctive in purpose clause introduced by *ut*

85.32 **neque litteras Graecas didici** hyperbolic. The near quotations of Lysias, Demosthenes, Isocrates, and Plato make this declaration "somewhat incongruous" (Skard 1941, 100). Marius must have learned at least elementary Greek as a young boy, since it was widely taught. For instance, Sallust tells us that Sulla was educated in Greek (*BI* 95.3). Rather than state a fact, Marius' denial conveys utter and complete disdain for Greek literature; cf. *BC* 25.2.

parum placebat eas discere explains the hyperbole: not that Marius didn't learn Greek, rather, he did not enjoy it. The antecedent of *eas* is *litteras* (pl. in Latin, sing. in English, "literature"); *litterae* is thus the implied subject of the pl. *profuerunt*.

quippe quae *quippe* with a rel. pron. introduces a causal clause with a sense of irony or sarcasm, "since *of course*"

ad uirtutem expresses purpose, "for prowess"

doctoribus i.e., the Greeks, dat. with intransitive *profuerunt*; *nihil* is adverbial acc., "since of course it was in no way advantageous to its teachers for prowess"

85.33 **illa** acc. pl. n., namely, the six infinitives

multo abl. of degree of difference with superl., as at *BI* 6.1

rei publicae dat. of advantage

hostem . . . tolerare Consistent word order emphasizes constancy of character. The first three infinitives (*ferire, agitare, metuere*) testify to Marius' bravery, the second three (*pati, requiescere, tolerare*) to his physical prowess in terms reminiscent of Catiline's extraordinary physical capacities, cf. *BC* 5.3.

ferire cf. *BI* 6.1, suggesting a metaphor of soldier as hunter, enemy as beast

agitare iterative with *praesidium* denotes a specific activity, "to keep watch or guard"

humi locative

85.34 **His . . . praeceptis** abl. of means

neque . . . neque connecting *colam* and *faciam*

illos arte . . . me opulenter parallel word order of prons. and advs.

gloriam meam, laborem illorum Marius promises not to take credit for his soldiers' work; on *labor militaris* and work as discipline, see Phang (2008, 201–47)

85.35 **Hoc . . . hoc** anaphora

ciuile imperium oxymoron

agas supply *uitam*; subjunctive in concessive clause introduced by *quom*, "although you live safely through softness"

exercitum supplicio cogere the transitive infinitive phrase is the subject of *est*, "to compel the army by punishment"

id grammatically unnecessary, for emphasis, "*this* is to be a master (i.e., of slaves), not a general." The words echo Isocrates' praise of Athens, *Panegyricus* 80, "desiring rather to be addressed as generals than as masters"

85.36 Note the finely balanced word order of this short sentence: *Haec atque alia talia* (objects) *maiores uostri* (subject) *faciundo* (transitive verbal) *seque remque publicam* (objects) *celebrauere* (transitive verb). The position of *maiores uostri* emphasizes their agency, "These and other such things, your ancestors, by doing"

faciundo abl. of means, transitive gerund with acc. objects, *haec atque alia talia*

85.37 **Quis** connecting rel. pron. = *quibus*, dat. with *freta*, antecedent *haec atque alia talia*

moribus dat. with *dissimilis*

illorum i.e., the *maiores*

85.38 **reliquere . . . reliquere** = *reliquerunt*

diuitias, imagines, memoriam sui praeclaram asyndeton of ascending tricolon in apposition to *omnia*; *sui* objective gen. On *memoria* in the *BI*, see Grethlein (2006, especially 140–43 on *memoria* in the speech of Marius and its echoes of the prologue).

poterant supply *relinquere*

dono dat. of purpose, "for a gift"

85.39 **Sordidum me** supply *esse* for indirect statement introduced by *aiunt*. The image of filth and dirt implied in *sordidum* is reminiscent of *BC* 23.6, *quasi pollui* and the stain brought upon the consulship by a *nouus homo*.

incultis moribus abl. of description, *uariatio* with the adj. *sordidum*: "they say that I am vulgar and of uncultivated habits"

scite adv.

conuiuium Aristocratic commanders and officers reclined at dinner, in keeping with their status as educated and refined men; by denying that he even knows how to give a banquet, Marius restrains himself from so much as the temptation to excessive consumption that corrupts others. On military dining, see Phang (2008, 249–84).

histrionem The Etruscan word for actor is *ister*, in Latin, *histrio*. According to Livy 7.2, when scenic entertainment was introduced at Rome (in the 360s), players were brought from Etruria to dance without singing or miming, making graceful movements. The young Romans began to copy them, at the same time making crude jokes in improvised verse with gestures to fit the words. According to Valerius Maximus, because this form of entertainment was eventually tempered by Roman austerity, the *histrio* was not kept from military service (*Memorable Deeds and Sayings* 2.4.4). Still, Marius denies having a *histrio* in his company.

pluris preti gen. of quality

coquom According to Livy 39.6.8–9 in his account of the year 187 (as Rome was developing into an imperialist power), "banquets became more elaborate and extravagant, and it was then that the cook (*coquus*), who had formerly the status of the lowest kind of slave, first acquired prestige, and what had once been a service-industry came to be thought of as an art." Thus, Marius' mention of a *coquus* suggests a phobia of Greek influence and an anxiety over an eroding Roman identity.

quam + compar. *pluris, coquom* and *uilicum* are syntactically equivalent

uilicum The *uilicus*, or overseer, on the other hand, holds an important managerial position on the Roman farm. According to Columella (*De Agricultura* 1.8.3–4), the ideal *uilicus* is possessed of energy and initiative; he is literate, diligent, and temperate. In short, it is a respectable occupation.

85.40   **Quae** connecting rel. pron., "These things"

confiteri open confession contrasts with sly irony

ex . . . ex anaphora

accepi governs three infinitives in indirect statement: *conuenire, oportere, esse*

munditias mulieribus, uiris laborem chiasmus, dats. with *conuenire*

omnibusque bonis dat. of possession; *-que* connects *conuenire* and *oportere*

gloriae . . . diuitiarum partitive gens. with *plus*

quam + compar. *plus*, tmesis

esse complementary infinitive with *oportere*, "it is fitting that all good men have more distinction than wealth"

decori dat. of purpose

85.41   **quod . . . quod** anaphora, antecedent *id*

faciant hortatory subjunctive

ament potent . . . agant . . . reliquant hortatory subjunctives that expand upon *faciant* in colorful detail

ubi . . . ibi correlatives

uentri et turpissumae parti corporis metonymy for food and sex; *uenter* refers to the belly as a receptacle for the indulgence of the appetite; *turpissumae parti corporis* is a circumlocution all the more conspicuous after the succinct—and graphic—*uentri*.

quibus dat. with *iucundiora*, antecedent *nobis*

epulis abl. of comparison

85.42 **flagitiis** abl. of means

turpissumi uiri, bonorum The antithesis not only underscores the difference in moral fiber, it also delivers a stinging insult because the same superl. was applied to *parti corporis*.

ereptum supine of purpose with *eunt*, "they proceed to seize upon the rewards of good men"

85.43 **artes** nom. in apposition to *luxuria et ignauia* and subject of *officiunt* and *sunt*; *artes* suggests learned behavior, and not innate qualities

illis dat. with *officiunt*

coluere = *coluerunt*, cf. *colam* 85.34; the nobility cultivates the worst practices, but Marius promises to cultivate his soldiers properly

nihil adverbial acc., "in no way"

officiunt . . . sunt the asyndeton implies a clipped adversative coordination, " . . . are in no way an obstacle to those who cultivate them but are . . ."

rei publicae innoxiae cladi double dat., "the ruin of the blameless Republic"

85.44-50 In his short summation (*peroratio*), Marius shifts from character (*mores*) to politics (*de re publica*). He urges his countrymen to enlist and then closes abruptly with a final jab at the nobility, whom he implies need longer speeches to muster courage.

85.44 **quoniam . . . respondi** marks the end of the *refutatio*, "since I have responded"

illis dat. indirect object

poscebant impf. denoting past action in progress, in rel. clause introduced by *quantum*, "how much my character, not their shameful acts (repeatedly) demanded"

pauca supply *uerba*; cf. *BC* 4.3, *BI* 17.1

85.45   **Primum omnium** followed by *Deinde*, 85.46

quae antecedent *omnia*

auaritiam, inperitiam atque superbiam in apposition to *omnia*, corresponding to Bestia, Albinus, and Metellus, without naming them

85.46   **locorum sciens** objective gen., "familiar with the terrain"

mehercule an interj. normally only used by men, derived from an apotropaic formula *ita me Hercules iuuet*, "thus may Hercules help me"

eius partitive gen., antecedent *exercitus*

auaritia aut temeritate abls. of means, alluding to the blunders of Bestia and Albinus

85.47   **Quam ob rem** connecting rel. pron., "on account of which," "for which reason" = "wherefore"

quibus militaris aetas dat. of possession, "who are of military age," men ages 17–46

capessite rem publicam frequentative suffix denotes a certain energy or eagerness of action, rather than its repetition, "be eager to engage in politics"

ex calamitate aliorum aut imperatorum superbia abls. of cause, chiasmus

neque . . . ceperit prohibitive subjunctive expressing a mild or polite command, "let fear not seize"

in agmine "on the march"

consultor . . . et socius in apposition to *egomet*

85.48   **dis iuuantibus** abl. absolute; the first mention of the gods in the speech

uictoria, praeda, laus asyndeton in apposition to *omnia*

Quae nom. pl. n., antecedent *omnia*, with adversative force, "But even if these things"

essent subjunctive in protasis of pres. contrary to fact condition

rei publicae dat. with *subuenire*

decebat the apodosis of the condition is indicative to express an air of certainty

85.49   **ignauia** abl. of means

forent . . . exigerent subjunctives in substantive clauses of purpose introduced by *uti . . . magis uti* and governed by *optauit*, strategically positioned between the two clauses

magis supply *quam*

boni honestique nom. pl. m. substantive adjs. in apposition to the subject (children), "as good and honorable men." By mentioning children again (as at 85.16), Marius touches upon an important theme of epideictic speeches: the education and well being of the city's youth. So it is appropriate that his words echo Plato's *Menexenus*, a funeral oration: "For they prayed not that their sons should become immortal, but valiant and renowned" (247d).

85.50   **dicerem** subjunctive apodasis of pres. contrary to fact condition

adderent subjunctive protasis of pres. contrary to fact condition

strenuis contrasts with *timidis*; cf. 85.46

abunde dictum supply *esse*. At the beginning of the *refutatio* (85.26), Marius uses *abunde* of his opponents, whom he anticipates would make an eloquent and carefully arranged speech (*abunde illis facundam et conpositam orationem*). The repetition suggests that Marius has proven himself as rhetorically competent as his opponents. The phrase also echoes *satis dictum*, though *abunde* is even stronger than *satis*. While the speech obviously stands apart from the narrative, still Sallust is able to incorporate his own voice; such *inuentio* characterizes speeches in ancient historiography.

Marius enlists soldiers, 86.1–3

Marius ignored property qualifications for military service and accepted as many volunteers as cared to come forward, regardless of their economic status. While the reform may have been no more than the product of a long-standing recruiting crisis, nevertheless it caused an abrupt (and distinct) change in the basic terms of service, resulting in strong allegiance to a general instead of the *res publica*. Marius thus began what was to become a prevailing—and perilous— trend in the late Republic, eventually culminating in the ascendancy of generals like Pompey and Caesar.

86.1   **Huiusce modi** All historians admit to a degree that the speeches in their works can only approximate what the speaker really said. Thucydides first formulated an explanation of his method of recording speeches, and phrases such as *huiusce modi* essentially allude to Thucydides 1.22 (see Introduction, xxxii).

        oratione habita abl. absolute

        conmeatu, stipendio, armis asyndeton, representing the haste (*propere*)

        cum his abl. of accompaniment

        A. Manlium Aulus Manlius, a legate of Marius

86.2   **scribere** simple historical infinitive depicts Marius' process as straightforward and uncomplicated, "Meanwhile, he himself enlisted soldiers"

        non more maiorum neque ex classibus Variation of the negatives (*non* and *neque*) and abl. without and with a prep. illustrate Marius' departure from traditional procedure, "not by the custom of our ancestors nor from the *classes*." King Servius is said to have divided the Roman citizens into five *classes* on the basis of property (Livy 1.43), and this was the standard for enlistment.

        sed introduces Marius' revolutionary alternatives to the old custom and the rules of property qualification

uti quoiusque lubido erat Instead of the *mos maiorum*, Marius depends on the fancy of each individual; *lubido* rarely carries a positive connotation.

capite censos Instead of *ex classibus*, Marius enlists "the members of a class by the head." Below Servius' five property classes were the *capite censi*, men with no property whatsoever, the poorest citizens with only their lives to give.

plerosque in apposition to *milites*

86.3   **Id factum** supply *esse* for indirect statement governed by *memorabant*

alii inopia bonorum, alii per ambitionem *inopia*, abl. of cause for *uariatio* with *per ambitionem*; parallel word order, "some because of a lack of good men, others because of ambition." Two explanations are given, but the second is surely meant to carry more weight.

quod conj., "because"

ab eo genere abl. of agent, "by that class"

et connects two causes in the *quod* clause

homini dat. of advantage, modified by transitive pple. *quaerenti*

egentissumus quisque "all the most needy," supply *erat* (the second cause in the *quod* clause); for *quisque* + superl., cf. *BC* 61.7, *BI* 84.2. At 85.15, Marius asserts that the bravest are the most noble; his detractors assert that the neediest are the most useful.

quoi dat. with *cara*, "to whom not even their own possessions are dear"

sua supply *sunt*; *sua* is nom. pl. n. substantive adj., "their own things," i.e., "possessions"

quippe quae supply dat. of possession *eis*, "because of course they have none" Sallust reflects the sarcasm of Marius' speech, cf. 85.5, 85.27, 85.32 (just as Marius had reflected Sallust's *breuitas*).

et connects (supplied *sunt*) and *uidentur* in the rel. clause introduced by *quoi*

omnia . . . honesta n. pl. subject, "to whom all things honorable seem (to come) with a price" This is the fourth time this notion is expressed in the *BI*. Sallust laments that "at Rome, everything is for sale" (*Romae omnia uenalia esse*, 8.1). Jugurtha is impressed by the fact that "at Rome, everything is for sale" (*quippe quoi Romae omnia uenire in animo haeserat*, 28.1). The only words uttered by Jugurtha in the entire monograph in *oratio recta* repeat the sentiment: "That is a city for sale and ready for ruin, if it finds a buyer" (*urbem uenalem et mature perituram, si emptorem inuenerit*, 35.10). For the importance of money to the characterization of Jugurtha, see Kraus 1999, 221–32.

ᗈ *Historiae*

The banquet of Metellus, 2.70

Quintus Caecilius Metellus Pius (praetor in 89, consul in 80) was the son of Metellus Numidicus, who waged war against Jugurtha. When Metellus Pius (hereafter simply referred to as Metellus) gained the advantage in a battle against Sertorius (see Introduction, xxvi), he allowed himself to be proclaimed *imperator*, and all the cities that he visited received him with altars and sacrifices. The excessive celebrations only made Metellus look foolish, since Sertorius had outwitted him on numerous occasions and still remained at large. No doubt Metellus' preposterousness is meant to contrast with the character of Pompey (see Introduction, xxvi–xxvii).

The Senate would decree a triumph to a victorious *imperator*, who would make a solemn entry into the city in a grand parade in Rome. The temples and buildings would be decorated and the streets crowded with spectators. The essential part of the triumph was the display of booty: weapons, standards, precious objects, and sacrificial victims. Next in the procession were the people: captives, followed by lictors (attendants allotted to Roman magistrates), and finally the soldiers in marching order and in full uniform. They sang a triumphal song laced with raunchy jokes at their general's expense. The banquet of Metellus mocks the features of the standard triumph (for a recent study of the Roman triumph, see Beard 2007).

While parts of the fragment are quoted by Nonius and Servius (see Introduction, xxv), the paragraph is recorded by Macrobius (*Saturnalia* 3.13.6–9), a Roman grammarian who lived in the late fourth century CE. He wrote the *Saturnalia*, seven books of dialogues held on the eve of the festival of Saturnalia. The participants include great thinkers of the time, among them Servius, the commentator on Vergil's *Aeneid*. The end of the third book is on luxury and the laws intended to curb it. Macrobius concludes the episode by calling Sallust the most severe critic and censor of foreign luxury (*Sallustius, grauissimus alienae luxuriae obiurgator et censor*); thus the fragment is testimony to Sallust's reputation as a stern moralist in late antiquity.

Valerius Maximus records the excessive honors of Metellus: "For what did Metellus Pius, a leading man of his times, want, when in Spain he allowed his arrival to be welcomed by his hosts with altars and incense? When he beheld, with glad heart, walls decked with golden tapestries? When he allowed most elaborate games to be alternated with immense banquets? When he attended dinner parties in palm-embroidered garments and received golden crowns let down from the ceilings on his head as if divine?" (*Memorable Deeds and Sayings*, 9.1.5).

ulteriorem Hispaniam the western of the two Roman provinces of the Iberian peninsula; see *BI* 19.4 on the two Spains

post annum "after a year," Metellus was proconsul in Further Spain in 75, so the year is 74.

concurrentium . . . omnium gen. pl. m.; within the gen. phrase are three adverbial modifiers: an adv. (*undique*), an adverbial acc. (*uirile et muliebre secus*), and a compound prepositional phrase (*per uias et tecta*)

uirile et mulibre secus The late-antique grammarians Nonius, Probus, and Charisius all preserve this phrase as evidence that the word *secus* is n. Roman historians rarely find it suitable for men and women to mingle in crowds.

Eum . . . uoluntate hyperbaton; these words belong in the *cum . . . inuitauerant* clause, "when the quaestor Gaius Urbinus and others, with his will known, invited him to dinner"

C. Vrbinus Gaius Urbinus, quaestor under Metellus in Further Spain in 74. Nothing else is known about him.

cognita uoluntate abl. absolute, suggesting that Metellus wanted excessive honors

ultra . . . morem "more than the convention of Romans and even of mortal men"

exornatis aedibus . . . scenisque . . . fabricatis abl. absolutes

aulaea such a Greek word offends Roman sensibility

ad ostentationem histrionum expresses purpose. The Romans had a peculiar distrust of, and distaste for, actors and their profession. Actors were regarded as no better than gladiators or prostitutes; they had practically no legal safeguards. The public display of one's body ran counter to the Roman value of *dignitas*, or personal dignity. Public performances had the potential to stir up crowds and incite public disorder; they were regarded as unseemly by the upper classes. On *histrio,* see *BI* 85.39.

croco a perfume made from the crocus used especially in theaters

sparsa supply *est*

in modum "in the manner of" (idiomatic with the acc.)

tum sedenti . . . tum uenienti dat. of respect and dat. with *supplicabatur,* i.e., Metellus

transenna abl. of means with *demissum.* The meaning of the word was a puzzlement to the grammarians. According to Nonius, it is a *fenestra*, or window; thus the statue would have been let down through a trap door of sorts. Servius translates it as *funis extentus*, or stretched rope.

Victoriae simulacrum Ancient statues of Victory were often winged, for example the Nike of Samothrace on display at the Louvre; so it is easy to imagine a winged figure descending from the ceiling.

cum machinato strepitu tonitruum abl. of accompaniment, "accompanied by the artificially produced sound of thunder." One can imagine a sort of *deus ex machina* as seen in theaters.

capiti dat. with *inponebat,* the subject is *simulacrum.* The statue places the crown on Metellus' head.

deo dat. with the impers. *supplicabatur,* "there was supplication with incense as if he were a god"

Toga picta embroidered garments worn by the triumphing general; Valerius Maximus (9.1.5, above) refers to *tunica palmata*, a flowered tunic worn under the toga by the triumphing generals.

plerumque adverbial acc.

amiculo . . . accumbenti for the double dat., see *BI* 6.2; the dat. sing. m. pres. pple. *accumbenti* is parallel with *sedenti* and *uenienti*.

quaesitissumae supply *erant*

neque . . . modo "not only"

prouinciam i.e., ulterior Hispania, further Spain

Mauretania on the nearness of Spain and Africa, cf. *BI* 18.5 and 18.9

plura genera in apposition to *epulae*

Quis rebus connecting rel. pron., abl. of means

dempserat Metellus is the subject

superba illa, grauia, indigna asyndeton; *illa*, acc. pl. n., object of *aestumantis*

Romano imperio abl. of specification with *indigna*

aestumantis acc. pl. m., transitive pple. modifying *uiros*. The episode thus recalls Sallust's general condemnation of moral decline that suffuses his works (see Earl 1961, especially 106).

Illustration Credits

1. Map of Rome, Showing the Location of the Gardens of Sallust: Adapted from Peter J. Aicher, *Rome Alive: A Source-Guide to the Ancient City*, Volume 1. © 2006 Bolchazy-Carducci Publishers, Inc.

2. Bust of Lucius Cornelius Sulla. Munich Glyptothek: Wikimedia Commons / Purchased in Rome

3. Bust of Marcus Tullius Cicero. Capitoline Museum, Rome, Italy: Wikimedia Commons / Glauco92

4. Cicero Denouncing Catiline. Cesare Maccari (1840–1919). Wall-painting, Palazzo Madama, Rome, Italy: Wikimedia Commons

5. Statue of Gaius Sallustius Crispus. Piazza Palazzo, L'Aquila, Italy: Lynn Anderson Images LLC

6. Map of Rome and the Mediterranean in the Late Republic. Mapping Specialists, Ltd. © 2009, Bolchazy-Carducci Publishers, Inc.

Appendix A

◌ *Time Line*

(Events Mentioned in This Volume)

218–201 BCE	Second Punic War
146	fall of Carthage, end of Third Punic War
133	Scipio Aemilianus sacks Numantia
118	death of Micipsa; Adherbal, Hiempsal, and Jugurtha joint rulers of Numidia
112	Jugurtha sacks Cirta
111–110	Bestia and Albinus campaign unsucessfully in Africa
109–108	Metellus Numidicus campaigns with some success in Africa
107	Marius' consulship and command in Africa
105	Bocchus of Mauretania surrenders Jugurtha to Sulla
104	Jugurtha exhibited in Marius' triumphal parade, then executed
86	Sallust born in Amiternum
82–81	dictatorship of Sulla, proscriptions
74	Metellus Pius proconsul in Further Spain
66	Catiline disbarred from candidacy for consulship
64	Catiline defeated in consular elections by Cicero
63	summer: Catiline defeated a second time in consular elections

	October 21	Senate passes the *senatus consultum ultimum*
	October 27	Manlius at Faesulae; Catiline to march on Rome
	November 6	conspirators meet at house of Marcus Porcius Laeca
	November 7	Cicero denounces Catiline in the Senate (*In Catilinam* 1)
	November 8	Cicero announces Catiline's departure to the people (*In Catilinam* 2)
	December 2	Cicero seizes ringleaders at the Mulvian Bridge
	December 3	Cicero discloses the conspiracy (*In Catilinam* 3)
	December 5	senatorial debate over punishment of conspirators (*In Catilinam* 4)
62	January	defeat of Catiline and his forces at Pistoria
61		Clodius on trial for profaning the Bona Dea festival
58		Cicero exiled
57		Cicero recalled
55/6		Sallust quaestor
52		Sallust tribune of the plebs
		Clodius murdered by band of Milo's supporters; riots at Rome
50		Sallust expelled from Senate
49		Sallust returned to Senate
		Sallust at Curicta
48		Sallust at Illyricum
47		Sallust at Campania

46	Sallust at Thapsus; governor of Africa Nova
45	Sallust accused of extortion
44	assassination of Caesar, Sallust begins writing history
43	establishment of triumvirate; proscriptions; murder of Cicero
42	Brutus and Cassius defeated at Philippi; *Bellum Catilinae* finished
39	*Bellum Iugurthinum* finished
36	Octavian defeats Sextus Pompey, Lepidus resigns
35	death of Sallust, *Historiae* unfinished

Appendix B

ର୍ଚ୍ଚ Map: Rome and the Mediterranean in the Late Republic

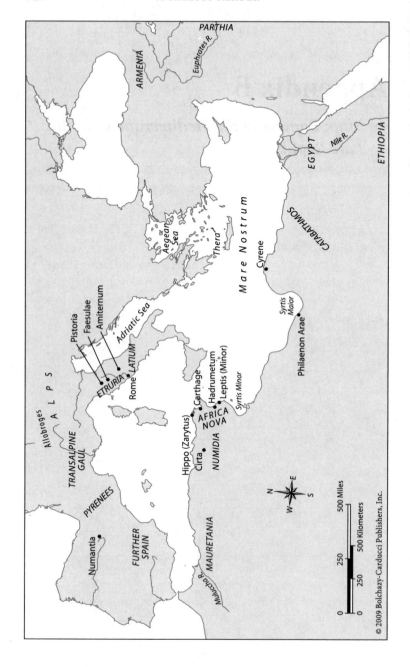

© 2009 Bolchazy-Carducci Publishers, Inc.

Vocabulary

A., Aulus

ā *or* **ab,** *prep.* + *abl.,* from, away from; by (*agent*)

abeō, -īre, -iī *or* **-iuī, -itum,** to go away, depart; to deviate, degenerate

abiūrō (1), to deny knowledge (of) falsely on oath

abnuō, -ere, -ī, —, to refuse to grant or provide

absoluō, -uere, -uī, -ūtum, to sum up, state briefly; to describe briefly

abstinentia, -ae, *f.,* restraint, self control

absum, abesse, āfuī, —, to be absent

absurdus, -a, -um, *adj.,* awkward, uncouth, uncivilized

abundē, *adv.,* fully, amply, with plenty to spare

ac. *See* **atque**

accipiō, -ere, -cēpī, -ceptum, to receive; to accept as valid; to learn, be told

accumbō, -ere, -cubuī, -cubitum, to lie down, recline

accūsō (1), to blame, find fault with

ācer, ācris, ācre, *adj.,* sharp, pointed, keen

aciēs, -ēī, *f.,* an army about to go into battle; battle formation

ācriter, *adv.,* strongly, violently, forcefully

actum, -ī, *n.,* achievement, exploit; (*pl.*) written record of events, gazette, record

ad, *prep.* + *acc.,* to, towards

adcēdō, -ere, -cessī, -cessum, to draw near, approach; to be added, be an additional factor

adcendō, -ere, -cendī, -censum, to burn, kindle

adciō, -īre, -cīuī, -cītum, to summon, send for, fetch

addō, -ere, addidī, additum, to bestow, add to

addūcō, -ere, -dūxī, -dūctum, to lead to, persuade

adeō, -īre, -iī *or* **-iuī, -itum,** to approach

adferrō, -ferre, attulī, allātum, to bring to; to generate

adfīnis, -is, *m.,* a relation by marriage, a relative in-law

adgredior, -ī, -gressus sum, to approach with hostile intent

ad hōc, *adv.,* in addition, furthermore

adhūc, *adv.,* up to the present time, as yet, so far, still

adigō, -ere, -ēgī, -actum, to cause (a person) to take (an oath)

adipiscor, -ī, adeptus sum, to obtain, acquire

adiungō, -ere, -iunxī, -iunctum, to get the support of, win over

administrō (1), to help, assist

adnītor, -ī, -nīsus sum, to try one's hardest, strive

adolescō, -ere, adolēuī, adultum, to become mature, grow up

adpetō, -ere, -petiī *or* **-petīuī, -petītum,** to seek the friendship of, cultivate as a friend; to try for, to desire for oneself

adrigō, -ere, -rexī, -rectum, to excite, arouse, stir

adrogō (1), to claim; to assume for oneself

adsciscō, -ere, -scīuī, -scītum, to take to oneself as an ally, admit, bring in

adsequor, -ī, -secūtus sum, to succeed in bringing about, achieve

adsīdō, -ere, -sēdī, —, to sit down

adsum, adesse, adfuī, —, to be present

adtendō, -ere, -tendī, -tentum, to observe, give attention to

adterō, -ere, -trīuī, -trītum, to wear away, diminish, waste, weaken

adtingō, -ere, -tigī, -tactum, to be contiguous to, be next to, adjoin; to touch upon, to mention briefly

adueniō, -īre, -uēnī, -uentum, to arrive; to set in, arise, develop

adulescens, -ntis, *m.,* a youthful person, a young man

adulescentia, -ae, *f.,* youth; youthfulness; the young

adulescentulus, -a, -um, *adj.,* very youthful, quite young

adultus, -a, -um, *adj.,* full-grown, adult, mature

aduocō (1), to summon

aduorsus, -a, -um, *adj.,* unfriendly, opposed, unfavorable; presented towards, directly facing (the enemy)

aedēs, aedis, *f.,* dwelling place; temple, sanctuary

aedificium, -iī, *n.,* building

aegrē, *adv.,* painfully, with difficulty

Aegyptus, -ī, *f.,* Egypt; (*pl.*) the Egyptians

aemulus, -ī, *m.,* competitor, rival

aequālis, -e, *adj.,* equal, similar

aequus, -a, -um, *adj.,* equal, fair

aerārium, -iī, *n.,* treasury

aes, aeris, *n.,* bronze; **aes alienum,** debt

aestās, -tātis, *f.,* summer

aestumō (1), to reckon

aestuō (1), to be agitated or restless; to seethe

aetās, -tātis, *f.,* an age group; persons of a particular age; age

aeternus, -a, -um, *adj.,* eternal, everlasting; immortal

Aethiops, -pis, *m.,* an inhabitant of Ethiopia, Ethiopian

Āfer, Āfra, Āfrum, *adj.,* African

Āfrica, -ae, *f.,* the continent of Africa

Africus, -a, -um, *adj.,* African

ager, agrī, *m.,* the land, fields

agitō (1), to rouse, stir up, provoke; **uītam agitāre,** to dwell

agmen, -inis, *n.,* marching column, battle array

agō, -ere, ēgī, actum, to do, drive, compel; to carry out, perform; **aetātem agere,** to live one's life; **tempus agere,** to spend time

agrestis, -e, *adj.,* rustic, rural; simple

āiō (*defective*), to say, affirm, assert

Albinus, -ī, *m.,* Albinus

algor, algōris, *m.,* coldness, cold

alibī, *adv.,* in another place, elsewhere

aliēnum, -ī, *n.,* the property or land of others

aliēnus, -a, -um, *adj.,* belonging to another, of another; unfavorable

aliquantus, -a, -um, *adj.,* a certain; (*pl.*) quite a lot of

aliquis, -qua, -quid, *pron.,* someone, anyone

aliquot, *indecl. adj.,* a number of, several, some

aliter, *adv.,* otherwise

alius, -a, -ud, *adj.,* other

Allobroges, -ogum, *m. pl.,* Allobroges, a tribe in Gaul

alter, -era, -erum, *pron.,* a second, another

altus, -a, -um, *adj.,* high; deep

alueus, -ī, *m.,* hull of a ship

ambiō, -īre, -iī *or* **-iuī, -ītum,** to visit in rotation, go round; to canvass for support

ambitiō, -ōnis, *f.,* a soliciting of votes, canvassing, rivalry for office; desire for advancement, ambition

amicītia, -ae, *f.,* friendship

amiculum, -ī, *n.,* clothing, dress

amīcus, -ī, *m.,* friend

āmitto, -ere, -mīsī, -missum, to dismiss; to lose

amō (1), to indulge in love

amor, amōris, *m.,* passion, love

amplector, -ī, amplexus sum, to embrace; to become devoted to or show fondness or favor toward

amplus, -a, -um, *adj.,* large, great

an, *conj.,* whether, or

anceps, -ipitis, *adj.,* uncertain, doubtful

anima, -ae, *f.,* breath, life; soul

animal, -ālis, *n.,* animal

animus, -ī, *m.,* mind, frame of mind; courage

annus, -ī, *m.*, year

ante, *prep.* + *acc.*, before, in front of

anteā, *adv.*, in the past, previously

anteeō, -īre, -iī *or* **-iuī, -itum,** to go before; to surpass

antehāc, *adv.*, in the past, before now

Antōnius, -iī, *m.*, Antonius

anxius, -a, -um, *adj.*, worried

aperiō, -īre, -uī, -ertum, to disclose, reveal, uncover, explain

appellō (1), to have or use as the name for, give the name to

apud, *prep.* + *acc.*, at, near, among, at the house of

aqua, -ae, *f.*, water

āra, -ae, *f.*, altar

arbor, arboris, *f.*, tree

arcessō, -ere, -īuī, -ītum, to summon, invite

ardens, -entis, *adj.*, eager, zealous, enthusiastic

ardor, ardōris, *m.*, fierce heat

arma, -ōrum, *n. pl.*, weapons, arms

armātus, -a, -um, *adj.*, defensively armed

Armenius, -iī, *m.*, an inhabitant of Armenia; (*pl.*) the people of Armenia

ars, artis, *f.*, art, skill; practice, pursuit

artē, *adv.*, strictly, in a stingy manner

artificium, -iī, *n.*, skill, cunning, contrivance

Asia, -ae, *f.*, the continent of Asia

asper, -era, -erum, *adj.*, harsh, rough, violent; difficult

asperitās, -tātis, *f.*, roughness, harshness, violence

aspernor, -ārī, aspernātus sum, to feel or show aversion for, scorn, reject

at, *conj.*, but, however, on the other hand

atque, *conj.*, and

atrōcitās, -tātis, *f.*, dreadfulness, savageness

atrox, -ōcis, *adj.*, terrible, frightful, cruel, savage

auāritia, -ae, *f.*, greed, gain, rapacity

auctor, auctōris, *m.*, originator, source, author (of information)

auctōritās, -tātis, *f.*, authority, impressiveness

audācia, -ae, *f.*, daring, boldness; impudence

audax, -ācis, *adj.*, daring, bold, confident; rash

audeō, -ēre, ausus sum, to dare

audiō, -īre, -iī *or* **-īuī, -ītum,** to hear

augeō, -ēre, auxī, auctum, to increase, grow; to advance; to elect

augescō, -ere, auxī, —, to increase in size, amount, number; to prosper

auidus, -a, -um, *adj.*, greedy

aulaeum, -ī, *n.*, the curtain of a theater; (*pl.*), curtains, hangings, tapestries

Aurēlia, -ae, *f.*, Aurelia

aut, *conj.*, or; aut . . . aut, either . . . or

autem, *adv.*, moreover, furthermore

auxilium, -iī, *n.*, help, aid, assistance; (*pl.*), auxiliary forces

barbarus, -a, -um, *adj.*, foreign

bellicōsus, -a, -um, *adj.*, warlike, fond of war

bellum, -ī, *n.*, war, warfare

bene, *adv.*, well, correctly, aptly, rightly

beneficium, -iī, *n.*, service, kindness, benefit

bestia, -ae, *f.*, beast, animal, creature

Bestia, -ae, *m.*, Bestia

Bocchus, -ī, *m.*, Bocchus, king of Mauretania

bonus, -a, -um, *adj.*, good, virtuous; bona, -ōrum, *n. pl.*, goods, property

breuis, -e, *adj.*, short, brief

Brūtus, -ī, *m.*, Brutus

C., Gaius

cadāuer, -eris, *n.*, dead body, corpse

cadō, -ere, cecidī, cāsum, to fall over, to fall to the ground

caedēs, -is, *f.*, killing, slaughter

caelum, -ī, *n.*, sky, heaven

Caesar, -aris, *m.*, Caesar

calamitās, -tātis, *f.*, disaster, misfortune, ruin, defeat

calor, calōris, *m.*, heat, heat of the sun, tropical heat

capessō, -ere, -īuī, -ītum, (with *rem publicam*), to engage in politics

capiō, -ere, cēpī, -tum, to take; to appropriate; to incur, suffer; consilium capere, to form a plan

caput, -itis, *n.*, head

carīna, -ae, *f.*, bottom of a ship, keel or hull

carō, -nis, *f.*, meat

carptim, *adv.*, selectively

Carthāginiensis, -e, *adj.*, Carthaginian

Carthāgo, -inis, *f.*, Carthage

cārus, -a, -um, *adj.*, dear, valued, costly

castra, -ōrum, *n. pl.*, camp

cāsus, -ūs, *m.*, chance; misfortune

Catabathmos, -oi, *m.*, (*Greek*) descent; the steep slope that separates Egypt and Cyrenaica

Catilīna, -ae, *m.*, Catiline

Catō, -ōnis, *m.*, Cato

causa, -ae, *f.*, cause, reason

causa, *prep.* + *gen.*, for the sake of, for the purpose of

-ce, *enclitic, added to demonstratives, deictic*

celeber, -bris, -bre, *adj.*, crowded; frequent; famed, distinguished

celebrō (1), to cause to be honored, confer distinction on

cēna, -ae, *f.,* dinner

censeō, -ēre, censuī, censum, to recommend

censor, censōris, *m.,* one who holds the office of the censor

census, -ūs, *m.,* members of a particular census class

cernō, -ere, crēuī, crētum, to discern, perceive

certō (1), to compete, contend, vie

certus, -a, -um, *adj.,* sure, certain, indisputable

cēterum, *adv.,* moreover, in addition; however that may be

cēterus, -a, -um, *adj.,* the rest, remaining

cibus, -ī, *m.,* food

cicātrix, -īcis, *f.,* scar

Cicerō, -ōnis, *m.,* Cicero

circumferō, -ferre, -tulī, -lātum, to pass around

circumueniō, -īre, -uēnī, -uentum, to surround, beset

citus, -a, -um, *adj.,* moving quickly; rapid

cīuīlis, -e, *adj.,* civil, of a citizen

cīuis, -is, *m.,* citizen

cīuitās, -tātis, *f.,* state; organized community of citizens

clādēs, -is, *f.,* calamity, disaster

clāmor, clāmōris, *m.,* shout, shouting

clāritūdō, -inis, *f.,* distinction, fame, renown

clārus, -a -um, *adj.,* distinct, well known, celebrated

classis, -is, *f.,* fleet; a body of citizens summoned for a levy; a class

clientēla, -ae, *f.,* the body of clients attached to a particular person; adherents

coepi, -isse, coeptum, to begin

coerceō, -ēre, -cuī, -citum, to compel, force, check, restrain

cognātus, -i, *m.,* kinsman

cognoscō, -ere, -gnōuī, -gnitum, to know, detect, become aware of

cōgō, -ere, coēgi, coactum, to reduce to a particular status; to bring back into order; to compel

cohors, -rtis, *f.,* cohort, a subdivision of a legion

colō, -ere, coluī, cultum, to till, cultivate, farm; to tend, look after

colōnia, -ae, *f.,* settlement or colony of citizens

colōs, colōris, *m.,* color, complexion

comitia, -iorum, *n. pl.,* elective assembly; election

comminus, *adv.,* at close quarters, hand to hand

commūnis, -e, *adj.,* shared, common, joint

complūrēs, -a, *adj. pl.,* a fair number, several, many

concēdō, -ere, -cessī, -cessum, to submit, defer, yield

concidō, -ere, -concidī, —, to fall down dying, collapse

concurrō, -ere, -currī,
-cursum, to come into large
numbers; to form a throng

concutiō, -ere, -cussī, -cussum,
to strike, upset, shake up

condō, -ere, -idī, -itum, to
found, establish

confertus, -a, -um, *adj.*,
crowded together,
thronging; united

conficiō, -ere, -fēcī, -fectum, to
accomplish, finish, conclude

confiteor, -ērī, -fessus sum, to
admit

conflō (1), to stir up, assemble;
to run up (a debt)

confodiō, -ere, -fōdī, -fossum,
to stab, wound fatally

coniungō, -ere, -iunxī,
-iunctum, to join together,
connect, unite

coniūratiō, -ōnis, *f.*, conspiracy

conmeātus, -us, *m.*, provisions,
supplies

conmercium, -iī, *n.*, trade

conmittō, -ere, -mīsī,
-missum, to commit,
perpetrate

conparō (1), to compare

conperiō, -īre, -ī, -itum, to find
out by investigation, learn,
ascertain

conpertus, -a, -um, *adj.*,
ascertained, proved

conpositus, -a, -um, *adj.*,
composed of, made from;
well arranged

conscientia, -ae, *f.*, sense of
guilt, guilty conscience

conscius, -a, -um, *adj.*,
conscious of guilt, having a
guilty conscience

consilium, -iī, *n.*, a plan, course
of action

conspiciō, -ere, -spexī,
-spectum, to catch sight of,
see

constantia, -ae, *f.*,
steadfastness, firmness of
character

constituō, -ere, -stituī,
-stitūtum, to place, locate;
to establish, create, decide

constō, -stāre, -stitī, —,
impers., it is apparent, plain,
established fact

consuescō, -ere, -suēuī,
-suētum, to become
accustomed or used to

consuētūdō, -inis, *f.*, habit;
intimacy, amorous
association

consul, -lis, *m.*, consul

consulāris, -e, *adj.*, having
been a consul, of consular
rank

consulātus, -us, *m.*, the office
of consul, consulship

consultor, -ōris, *m.*, advisor,
counselor

contemnō, -ere, -tempsī,
-temptum, to scorn, regard
with contempt

contendō, -ere, -tendī,
-tentum, to compete,
contend

conterō, -ere, -trīuī, -trītum, to
spend, use up

contiō, -ōnis, *f.,* public meeting, assembly

contrā, *prep.* + *acc.,* opposite, against, in opposition to

contrā, *adv.,* contrarywise, otherwise, differently;
contra ac, otherwise than, contrary to

cōnūbium, -iī, *n.,* intermarriage; marriage

conueniō, -īre, -uēnī, -uentum, to be becoming to, befit

conuertō, -ere, -uertī, -uersum, to turn one's face toward a given object

conuīuium, -iī, *n.,* dinner party

conuocō (1), to summon together, assemble

cooperiō, -īre, -operuī, -opertum, to cover completely

cōpia, -ae, *f.,* abundance, supply; (*pl.*), troops, forces

coquus, -ī, *m.,* a cook

Cornēlius, -iī, *m.,* Cornelius

corōna, -ae, *f.,* wreath of flowers, especially for festive occasions

corpus, -oris, *n.,* body

corrumpō, -ere, -rūpī, -ruptum, to damage, corrupt, render morally unsound

crēdibilis, -e, *adj.,* capable of being believed, conceivable

crēditum, -ī, *n.,* a loan or debt

crēdō, -ere, -idī, -itum, + *dat.,* to trust, believe, rely on

crescō, -ere, crēuī, crētum, to increase, gain influence

crocum, -ī, *n.,* saffron, as a perfume

cultor, -ōris, *m.,* inhabitants, growers

cum, *conj.,* when; + *subjunctive* since, although

cum, *prep.* + *abl.,* with

cunctus, -a, -um, *adj.,* whole, all

cupidē, *adv.,* eagerly, hastily

cupiditās, -tātis, *f.,* passionate desire, longing, desire for wealth

cupīdō, -inis, *m./f.,* passionate desire, longing, lust

cupidus, -a, -um, *adj.,* eager, desirous, longing

cupiens, -ntis, *adj.,* desirous, eager, anxious

cupiō, -ere, -iī *or* **-īuī, -ītum,** to wish for, want, desire

cūra, -ae, *f.,* anxiety, worry, care, concern

Curius, -iī, *m.,* Curius

cūrō (1), to watch over, care for

cursus, -ūs, *m.,* running

Cȳrēnē, -ēs, *f.,* Cyrene, a town of northwest Libya

D., Decimus

dē, *prep.* + *abl.,* about, down, down from

dēbeō (2), to owe, be obliged to, ought

dēcernō, -ere, -crēuī, -crētum, to determine, decide

decet, decuit, *impers.,* it is fitting, right, proper

dēclārō (1), to announce, declare, tell

dēclīuis, -e, *adj.,* sloping
downwards

decōrus, -a, -um, *adj.,*
handsome, good looking

decus, -oris, *n.,* high esteem,
honor, glory, distinction,
dignity; (*pl.*) honorable
achievements, exploits

dēdecorō (1), to bring discredit
on, dishonor, disgrace

dēdō, -ere, dedidī, deditum, +
dat., to surrender

dēgustō (1), to take a taste of,
eat or drink a little of

dehinc, *adv.,* after that,
thereupon; next, then

dein. *See* **deinde**

deinceps, *adv.,* in succession, in
turn, next

deinde, *adv.,* then, next

dēlinquō, -ere, -līquī, -lictum,
to fall short

dēmittō, -ere, -mīsī, -missum,
to let fall, drop, cause to
descend

dēmō, -ere, dempsī, demptum,
to remove, take off, take
away

dēnegō (1), to deny

dēnique, *adv.,* finally, at last, at
length, lastly

dēserō, -ere, -seruī, -sertum, to
desert, fail, abandon, quit

dēsidia, -ae, *f.,* idleness,
inactivity

**despiciō, -ere, -spexī,
-spectum,** to look down on

dētineō, -ēre, -tinuī, -tentum,
to keep (from an activity)

dētrīmentum, -ī, *n.,* harm,
damage, loss

deus, deī, *m.,* god

dīcō, -ere, dixī, dictum, to say

dīctitō (1), to persist in saying,
repeat

dictum, -ī, *n.,* word

diēs, diēī, *m.,* day, daylight

difficilis, -e, *adj.,* hard,
troublesome, difficult

difficultās, -tātis, *f.,* difficulty

dignitās, -tātis, *f.,* worthiness,
excellence, rank, esteem,
dignity

dignus, -a, -um, *adj.,*
appropriate, suitable,
worthy

dīgredior, -ī, -gressus sum, to
go off, depart, separate

dīlābor, -ī, -lapsus sum, to fall
to pieces

dīmittō, -ere, -mīsī, -missum,
to send away, dismiss

discēdō, -ere, -cessī, -cessum,
to disperse

discernō, -ere, -crēuī, -crētum,
to distinguish, separate

discō, -ere, didicī, —, to learn

discordia, -ae, *f.,* dissension,
difference of opinion

disiciō, -ere, -iēcī, -iectum, to
scatter

**dissentiō, -īre, -sensī,
-sensum,** to differ in
opinion, disagree

disserō, -ere, -seruī, -sertum,
to set out in words, treat

dissimilis, -e, *adj.,* unlike,
different

dissimulātor, -ōris, *m.,* one who conceals his purpose, a dissembler

dissoluō, -ere, -soluī, -solūtum, to deprive of strength, weaken, wear out

diū, *adv.,* for a long time

dīues, -itis, *adj.,* wealthy, rich

dīuidō, -ere, -uīsī, -uīsum, to divide, separate

dīuīsiō, -ōnis, *f.,* division into parts, separation

dīuitiae, -ārum, *f. pl.,* wealth, riches

dīuorsē, *adv.,* in different directions, differently

dīuorsus, -a, -um, *adj.,* opposed

dō, dare, dedī, datum, to give

doceō, -ēre, docuī, doctum, to tell, inform, demonstrate, show, teach

doctor, doctōris, *m.,* teacher

doctus, -a, -um, *adj.,* learned, wise, expert; skilled in

doleō (2), to suffer pain, grieve; to be a cause of pain or grief, rankle, annoy

dolor, dolōris, *m.,* pain, distress, anguish, grief

dolus, -ī, *m.,* trickery, treachery, cunning

dominātiō, -ōnis, *f.,* position of absolute authority, dominion

dominus, -ī, *m.,* despot, supreme ruler, lord

domus, -ūs *or* **-ī,** *m./f.,* house, home

dōnum, -ī, *n.,* gift; **dōna mīlitāria,** prizes awarded to soldiers for distinguished service

dubitō (1), to be in doubt, be uncertain

dubius, -a, -um, *adj.,* uncertain, doubtful

dūcō, -ere, duxī, ductum, to lead; to consider, believe, think

dum, *conj.,* as long as, while, until; + *subjunctive,* provided that

duo, -ae, -o, *adj.,* two

dux, ducis, *m.,* leader

ē *or* **ex,** *prep.* + *abl.,* out, from, after, because of

effētus, -a, -um, *adj.,* worn out with child bearing

effugiō, -ere, -fūgī, —, to flee, escape, avoid

egens, -ntis, *adj.,* poverty stricken, needy, indigent

egestās, -tātis, *f.,* extreme poverty, need, destitution

ego, *pron.,* I

ēgregius, -a, -um, *adj.,* outstanding, illustrious

ēleganter, *adv.,* attractively, elegantly, properly

ēloquentia, -ae, *f.,* ability to express oneself in words; eloquence

ēmereō (2), to earn

emō, -ere, ēmī, emptum, to buy, purchase

ēnitescō, -ere, -nituī, —, to become conspicuously evident, stand out ēnuntiō (1), to disclose; to pronounce

eō, īre, iī *or* īuī, ītum, to go; + *supine*, to go for a specified purpose

eō, *adv.*, to that place, there

eōdem, *adv.*, to the same purpose

epulae, -ārum, *f. pl.*, sumptuous meal, feast, banquet

eques, -itis, *m.*, cavalryman, (*pl.*) cavalry; member of equestrian order

equidem, *adv.*, with *ego* implied: I for my part, personally speaking

equitō (1), to ride horseback

ergō, *adv.*, for that reason, therefore

ēripiō, -ere, -ripuī, -reptum, to seize, pull, take by force

errō (1), to wander, stray

et, *conj.*, and; et . . . et, both . . . and

etenim, *conj.*, and indeed, the fact is, for

etiam, *adv.*, still, yet, even now; etiam atque etiam, more and more, incessantly, ever more urgently (*with verbs of entreaty*)

Etrūria, -ae, *f.*, Etruria

ēueniō, -īre, -uēnī, -uentum, to happen, come about, turn out

Eurōpa, -ae, *f.*, the continent of Europe

exagitō (1), to arouse, agitate, stir up

exciō, -īre, -cīuī, -cītum, to rouse, start, stir into action

execrātiō, -ōnis, *f.*, the act of cursing, imprecation, curse

exequor, -ī, execūtus sum, to follow; to carry out

exerceō (2), to train, practice

exercitus, -ūs, *m.*, army

exigō, -ere, -ēgī, -actum, to spend a period of time, pass time

existumō (1), to value, esteem, judge; to think, suppose

exitus, -ūs, *m.*, result, issue, outcome

exoptō (1), to long for

exornō (1), to adorn, decorate, beautify

expectō (1), to expect, hope for

expedītus, -a, -um, *adj.*, (of troops) ready for action; lightly armed

explānō (1), to make clearly intelligible, expound, explain

expleō, -ēre, -plēuī, -plētum, to fill; to satisfy the demands or appetites of

explōrō (1), to ascertain

expōnō, -ere, -posuī, -positum, to set forth in words, relate, describe, explain

exsanguis, -e, *adj.*, lacking blood, bloodless

extollō, -ere, —, —, to lift up, raise, praise, extol

exūrō, -ere, -ussī, -ustum, to make dry, parch

Fabius, -iī, *m.*, Fabius

fabricō (1), to construct, build, devise

facētiae, -ārum, *f. pl.,* wit; the quality of being witty or facetious

faciēs, faciēī, *f.,* outward appearance, looks

facilis, -e, *adj.,* easy, straightforward

facilitās, -tātis, *f.,* ease of performance, fluency, propensity

facinus, -oris, *n.,* deed, achievement; crime, outrage

faciō, -ere, fēcī, factum, to make, do

factiō, -ōnis, *f.,* political party; partisanship

factiōsus, -a, -um, *adj.,* belonging to a faction; having powerful connections

factum, -ī, *n.,* deed, action

fācundia, -ae, *f.,* eloquence

fācundus, -a, -um, *adj.,* eloquent, fluent

Faesulae, -arum, *f. pl.,* Faesulae, a town in Etruria

Faesulānus, -a, -um, *adj.,* of or belonging to Faesulae

fallō, -ere, fefellī, -sum, to decieve, mislead

falsus, -a, -um, *adj.,* erroneous, untrue, false

fāma, -ae, *f.,* news, report, rumor, public opinion, reputation

familiāris, -e, *adj.,* private, personal, belonging to one's family; **res familiāris,** one's private property, estate

fās, *defective noun,* right, that which is fitting, in accordance with law

fateor, -ērī, fassus sum, to admit, profess, declare

fatīgō (1), to tire, weary, exhaust

faueō, -ēre, fāuī, fautum, + *dat.,* to show favor to, side with, approve of

fēlix, -īcis, *adj.,* lucky, auspicious, blessed, fortunate

fera, -ae, *f.,* wild animal, beast

ferē, *adv.,* practically, almost, nearly

ferentārius, -iī, *m.,* a soldier armed with missile weapons only; a skirmisher

ferīnus, -a, -um, *adj.,* of wild beasts

feriō, -īre, —, —, to strike, strike down or kill

ferō, ferre, tulī, lātum, to carry, bring, bear, endure

ferōcia, -ae, *f.,* fierceness

ferōciter, *adv.,* fiercely, ferociously, aggressively

ferox, -ōcis, *adj.,* having a violent or savage nature, fierce

ferrum, -ī, *n.,* iron; sword

fertilis, -e, *adj.,* fruitful, productive, rich or abounding in

festīnō (1), to hasten, hurry

fidēs, -ēī, *f.,* trust; allegiance, loyalty

fīdus, -a, -um, *adj.,* keeping faith, faithful, loyal, devoted

fīlius, -iī, *m.,* son

fingō, -ere, finxī, fictum, to make up, fabricate, invent

fīnis, -is, *m.,* boundary, border, outermost limit

fīnitumus, -a, -um, *adj.,* neighboring, near by, adjacent

fīō, fierī, factus sum, to take place, occur, come about, become; to be elected

flāgitiōsus, -a, -um, *adj.,* disgraceful, shocking, scandalous

flāgitium, -iī, *n.,* disgrace, scandal, shameful act

flūmen, -inis, *n.,* river or stream

foedus, -a, -um, *adj.,* repulsive in appearance, hideous, ugly

fore. *See* **sum**

forīs, *adv.,* in one's public life; abroad

forma, -ae, *f.,* appearance, beauty

forte, *adv.,* by chance

fortis, -e, *adj.,* strong

fortūna, -ae, *f.,* fortune, favorable chance, opportunity

fortūnātus, -a, -um, *adj.,* attended by good fortune, fortunate, lucky

forum, -ī, *n.,* public square, center of town, forum

frequentō (1), to populate

fretum, -ī, *n.,* narrow strait, channel

frētus, -a, -um, *adj. + dat.,* relying on, confident of

frūges, -ūgum, *f. pl.,* crops

frustrā, *adv.,* to no purpose, in vain, without avail

fuga, -ae, *f.,* flight, rout

Fuluia, -ae, *f.,* Fulvia

fundō, -ere, fūdī, fūsum, to pour, pour out; to route, disperse

furor, furōris, *m.,* violent madness, delirium

Gabīnius, -iī, *m.,* Gabinius

Gaetūlus, -a, -um, *adj.,* Gaetulian

Gallia, -ae, *f.,* Gaul

Gallicus, -a, -um, *adj.,* Gallic, of Gaul

Gallus, -ī, *m.,* an inhabitant of Gaul, a Gaul

gaudium, -iī, *n.,* joy, delight

generōsus, -a, -um, *adj.,* noble, superior

gens, gentis, *f.,* nation, people, group

genus, -eris, *n.,* stock, descent, birth, origin; social or political class or group

gerō, -ere, gessī, gestum, to wage, manage; **bellum gerere,** to wage war

gignō, -ere, genuī, genitum, to bring into being; (*pass.*) to be born

gladius, -iī, *m.,* sword

globus, -ī, *m.,* band, clique, close association

glōria, -ae, *f.,* glory, distinction

glōrior, -ārī, gloriātus sum, to boast

Graecus, -a, -um, *adj.,* Greek

grandis, -e, *adj.,* great in amount or number, large

grātia, *prep.* + *gen.,* on account of, for the sake of, because of

grātuītō, *adv.,* without payment, for nothing

grātus, -a, -um, *adj.,* acceptable, welcome, popular, favorable

grauis, -e, *adj.,* troublesome, obnoxious; grave, serious

grauiter, *adv.,* heavily, seriously

habeō (2), to have, hold; (*pass.*) to be considered

Hadrumetum, -ī, *n.,* Hadrumetum

hasta, -ae, *f.,* spear

haud, *adv.,* not, scarcely, without a doubt

Herculēs, -eī, *m.,* Hercules

hērēditās, -tātis, *f.,* inheritance

hic, haec, hoc, *pron.,* this

Hiempsal, -lis, *m.,* Hiempsal

hiems, hiemis, *f.,* winter

Hippō, -ōnis, *m.,* Hippo Zarytus

Hispānia, -ae, *f.,* Spain, the Spanish peninsula

histriō, -ōnis, *f.,* an actor or performer in a pantomime

homō, hominis, *m.,* man; human being

honestē, *adv.,* honorably, with propriety

honestus, -a, -um, *adj.,* regarded with respect, well born, honorable, respectable

honor, honōris, *m.,* high esteem, respect; political office

hortor, -ārī, hortātus sum, to incite to action, encourage

hospes, hospitis, *m.,* guest, visitor

hostīlis, -e, *adj.,* of or belonging to the enemy, enemy

hostis, -is, *m.,* enemy

hūc, *adv.,* to this place, hither

hūmānus, -a, -um, *adj.,* of or belonging to human beings; human

humus, -ī, *f.,* the ground

iaculor, -ārī, iaculātus sum, to throw a javelin

iam, *adv.,* at this point, now, already; **iam prīmum,** *adv.,* to begin with, first of all

iānua, -ae, *f.,* door

ibi, *adv.,* in that place, there; therein

īdem, eadem, idem, *pron.,* the same

igitur, *conj.,* in that case, then; consequently, therefore

ignārus, -a, -um, *adj.,* having no knowledge, ignorant, unaware (of); having no experience of

ignāuia, -ae, *f.,* sloth, idleness, lack of spirit

ignōrō (1), to be unaware

ignoscō, -ere, ignōuī, ignōtum, to forgive, pardon

ille, illa, illud, *pron.,* that

imāgō, -inis, *f.,* death mask; (*pl.*) the masks that represent noble ancestry; nobility

immoderātus, -a, -um, *adj.,* measureless, boundless, unrestrained

imperātor, -ōris, *m.,* commander, general

imperitō (1), to be in command; to exercise control over

imperium, -iī, *n.,* supreme power, rule

imperō (1), to hold political power, rule

in, *prep.* + *abl.,* in, on, in the case of; + *acc.,* into, onto, towards, against

inbēcillus, -a, -um, *adj.,* weak, feeble, lacking in moral strength

incēdō, -ere, -cessī, —, to march forward, advance

incendium, -iī, *n.,* fire

incendō, -ere, -cendī, -censum, to set on fire

inceptum, -ī, *n.,* undertaking, enterprise, attempt

incertus, -a, -um, *adj.,* uncertain, not yet decided

incessus, -ūs, *m.,* the action or act of walking, gait

incitō (1), to arouse, evoke, encourage, incite

incognitus, -a, -um, *adj.,* unfamiliar, strange

incola, -ae, *m.,* inhabitant

incrēdibilis, -e, *adj.,* impossible or difficult to believe, unbelievable

increpō (1), to rebuke

incruentus, -a, -um, *adj.,* not stained with blood, without bloodshed

incultē, *adv.,* without refinement of manners, coarsely

incultus, -a, -um, *adj.,* rough, coarse, lacking in culture

incurrō, -ere, -currī, -cursum, to rush in or charge, run into

incuruus, -a, -um, *adj.,* curved, bent

inde, *adv.,* from that place, thence

indignus, -a, -um, *adj.,* beneath the dignity of, unbecoming, unworthy

indūcō, -ere, -duxī, -ductum, to lead into; **indūcere in animum,** to receive an idea into the mind, admit to consideration

industrius, -a, -um, *adj.,* diligent, active

inedia, -ae, *f.,* starvation, fasting

inertia, -ae, *f.,* idleness, sloth, indolence

infēcundus, -a, -um, *adj.,* infertile, unfruitful

inferior, -ius, *compar. adj.,* lower

infestus, -a, -um, *adj.,* hostile

infirmus, -a, -um, *adj.,* weak, fragile

ingenium, -iī, *n.,* natural disposition, temperament; intellect

ingens, -ntis, *adj.,* huge, vast
ingenuus, -a, -um, *adj.,* free-born
inimīcus, -a, -um, *adj.,* unfriendly, enemy
iniquus, -a, -um, *adj.,* prejudiced
initium, -iī, *n.,* beginning, start, commencement
iniūria, -ae, *f.,* wrong, injustice
iniustē, *adv.,* unjustly
inmortālis, -e, *adj.,* immortal, everlasting
innocens, -ntis, *adj.,* blameless, innocent
innocentia, -ae, *f.,* freedom from guilt, innocence; integrity
innoxius, -a, -um, *adj.,* blameless, innocent
inopia, -ae, *f.,* lack, deficiency
inparātus, -a, -um, *adj.,* unready, unprepared
inpellō, -ere, -pulī, -pulsum, to compel to, urge
inpendeō, -ēre, impensus sum, to impend, threaten
inperītia, -ae, *f.,* ignorance
inpiger, inpigra, inpigrum, *adj.,* energetic, brisk
inpōnō, -ere, -posuī, -positum, to put on
inportuōsus, -a, -um, *adj.,* having no harbors
inprōuīsus, -a, -um, *adj.,* unforeseen, unexpected
inpūrus, -a, -um, *adj.,* morally foul, vile
inquam (*defective*), to say (introduces direct speech)

insidiae, -ārum, *f. pl.,* ambush, trap, plot
insigne, -is, *n.,* decoration, mark of honor
insolens, -ntis, *adj.,* unaccustomed
insolentia, -ae, *f.,* lack of moderation, extravagance
insomnium, -iī, *n.,* (usually *pl.*), wakefulness, sleeplessness
instituō, -ere, instituī, institūtum, to establish
instō, -āre, -stitī, -statum, + *dat.,* to press in a hostile manner; to loom, threaten
instrūmentum, -ī, *n.,* equipment
insum, inesse, infuī, —, to be in or on
integer, integra, integrum, whole; uninjured
integritās, -tātis, *f.,* soundness, wholeness, moral uprightness
intellegō, -ere, intellexi, intellectum, to understand, realize
intempestus, -a, -um, *adj.,* unseasonable; **intempesta nox,** the dead of night
intendō, -ere, -tendī, -tentum, to apply oneself, direct one's energy to
inter, *prep.* + *acc.,* among, amid
interdum, *adv.,* at times, in the meantime, meanwhile
intereā, *adv.,* meanwhile, in the meantime
intereō, -īre, -iī *or* **īuī, -itum,** to die, perish, be killed

interficiō, -ere, -fēcī, -fectum, to do away with, put to death, kill

interim, *adv.,* meanwhile

interpretor, -ārī, interpretātus sum, to give an account of, explain; to expound in another language, translate

intestīnus, -a, -um, *adj.,* civil, domestic, internal

intrā, *prep.* + *acc.,* within; toward, without passing beyond, on this side of

introeō, -īre, -iī *or* **-īuī, -itum,** to go inside, enter

inuādō, -ere, -uasī, -uasum, to seize possession of, attack

inuideō, -ēre, -uīdī, -uīsum, + *dat.,* to begrudge, refuse; to envy

inuidia, -ae, *f.,* jealousy, envy, spite, dislike

inuidus, -a, -um, *adj.,* envious, jealous, grudging

inuītō (1), to invite to entertainment

inuortō, -ere, -uortī, -uorsum, to turn upside down

iocus, -ī, *m.,* joke, jest, sport

ipse, ipsa, ipsud, *adj.,* himself, herself, itself

is, ea, id, *pron.,* he, she, it; this, that

iste, ista, istud, that; (*pejorative*) that dastardly

ita, *adv.,* expressing degree: to that extent, so, thus

Italia, -ae, *f.,* Italy, the Italian peninsula

item, *adv.,* in the same manner, similarly, likewise

iubeō, -ēre, iussī, iussum, to order

iūcundus, -a, -um, *adj.,* pleasant, agreeable

iūdicium, -iī, *n.,* legal proceedings, case

Iugurtha, -ae, *m.,* Jugurtha

Iugurthīnus, -a, -um, *adj.,* of or relating to Jugurtha

iūs iurāndum, *n.,* a binding formula to be sworn to; an oath

iūs, iūris, *n. sing.,* authority, right, jurisdiction

iussus, -ūs, *m.,* command

iuuentūs, -tūtis, *f.,* young men collectively; youth

iuuō, -āre, iūuī, iūtum, to help, promote, benefit, do good

iuxtā, *adv.,* alike, equally as much

L., Lucius

labor, labōris, *m.,* work, labor, toil

laborō (1), to work, toil, labor, strive

lacerō (1), to mutilate; to attack with abuse or accusations

Laeca, -ae, *m.,* Laeca

laedō, -ere, laesī, laesum, to inujure, damage, harm

laetitia, -ae, *f.,* gladness, delight

laetus, -a, -um, *adj.,* cheerful, glad, happy

largior, -īrī, largītus sum, to bestow, lavish

largītiō, -ōnis, *f.,* largess, extravagant gifts; bribery

Latīnus, -a, -um, *adj.,* Latin

lātitūdō, -inis, *f.,* wide area, large extent

Latium, -iī, *n.,* Latium

latrō, -ōnis, *m.,* brigand, robber, bandit

latus, -eris, *n.,* side

laudō (1), to praise

laus, laudis, *f.,* praise

lēgātus, -ī, *m.,* ambassador, envoy, representative, delegate

legiō, -ōnis, *f.,* legion

legō, -ere, lēgī, lectum, to read

lēniō, -īre, -iī *or* **-īuī, -ītum,** to alleviate, mitigate, mollify

leō, -ōnis, *m.,* lion

lepos, lepōris, *m.,* charm, grace, attractiveness; wit, humor

Leptis, -is, *f.,* Leptis Minor

lex, lēgis, *f.,* law

līber, libera, liberum, free

liber, -brī, *m.,* book

līberī, -ōrum, *m. pl.,* children

liberō (1), + *abl.,* to deliver, release, free from

Libyē, -ēs, *f.,* Libya, its peoples

licet, licuit, *impers.,* it is allowed, permitted

lingua, -ae, *f.,* tongue; language

litterae, -arum, *f. pl.,* literature

locum *or* **locus, -ī,** *n./m.,* place, spot, position; opportunity, position in society, rank

locuplēs, -ētis, *adj.,* wealthy, rich

longē, *adv.,* a long way, far, at a distance, far off

loquor, -ī, locūtus sum, to talk, speak

lubet, lubuit, *impers.,* it is pleasing or agreeable

lubīdō, -inis, *f.,* desire, longing, wish, fancy; lust

luctus, -ūs, *m.,* mourning

lūmen, -inis, *n.,* light

luxuria, -ae, *f.,* licentiousness, indulgence, luxury, extravagance

luxus, -ūs, *m.,* indulgence, luxury

M., Marcus

māchinātus, -a, -um, *adj.,* artificially produced

maeror, -ōris, *m.,* grief, sorrow, mourning

magis, *adv.,* to a greater extent, more, rather

magistrātus, -ūs, *m.,* magistracy, office of a magistrate

magnificus, -a, -um, *adj.,* splendid

magnitūdō, -inis, *f.,* vast size, great size

magnus, -a, -um, *adj.,* great in size or extent, big

maior, -us, *compar. adj.,* greater

maiorēs, -um, *m. pl.,* ancestors

maledictum, -ī, *n.,* insult, reproach, taunt

maleficus, -a, -um, *adj.,* harmful, noxious, injurious, baneful

mālō, malle, maluī, —, to prefer

malus, -a, -um, *adj.,* nasty, bad, unpleasant; wicked, evil

mandō (1), to commit, entrust

Manlius, -iī, *m.,* Manlius

mansuētūdō, -inis, *f.,* tameness, gentleness, clemency

manufestus, -a, -um, *adj.,* plainly guilty, caught red-handed

manus, -ūs, *f.,* an armed force, a band

mapālia, -ium, *n. pl.,* huts in which nomadic Africans lived; nomadic settlements

mare, maris, *n.,* the sea

maritumus, -a, -um, *adj.,* of or belonging to the sea, maritime

Marius, -iī, *m.,* Marius

matēria, -ae, *f.,* wood, timber; matter, material

mātūrē, *adv.,* quickly, in good time, early

mātūrō (1), to perform or finish in good time; to hasten

Maurētānia, -ae, *f.,* a country of North Africa

Maurus, -a, -um, *adj.,* of or belonging to the Mauri, Moorish, Moroccan

maxumē, *adv.,* to the greatest extent, very much

maxumus, -a, -um, *superl. adj.,* greatest

mediocris, -e, *adj.,* of medium size or amount, moderate, average

medius, -a, -um, *adj.,* central, middle; the middle of

Mēdus, -a, -um, *adj.,* of or belonging to the Medes, Median

mehercule, *interj.,* By Hercules!

melius, *compar. adv.,* better

memor, -oris, *adj.,* mindful

memorābilis, -e, *adj.,* worthy of being recorded; remarkable

memoria, -ae, *f.,* memory; what is remembered of a person or thing, repute

memorō (1), to narrate, relate, tell; to recall to mind

mens, mentis, *f.,* mind, thought

mercēs, mercēdis, *f,* wage, fee, reward, payment

meritum, -ī, *n.,* worthiness to receive good treatment

-met, *enclitic, adds emphasis to prons.*

Metellus, -ī, *m.,* Metellus

metuō, -ere, -ī, —, to regard with fear, be afraid of

metus, -ūs, *m.,* fear

meus, -a, -um, *poss. pron.,* my

Micipsa, -ae, *m.,* Micipsa

mīles, -itis, *m.,* soldier; **mīlitēs scrībere,** to draft an army

mīlitāris, -e, *adj.,* of or connected with the army, military

mīlitia, -ae, *f.,* the military, military service

mīlitō (1), to serve as a soldier, perform military service

minimum, *adv.,* in the least degree

minor, -ārī, minātus sum, to threaten

minor, -us, *compar. adj.,* smaller; younger

minuō, -ere, minuī, minūtum, to reduce, lessen, abate

minus, *compar. adv.,* to a smaller degree, less

misceō, -ēre, miscuī, mixtum, to mix, blend

misereor, -ērī, miseritus sum, + *gen.,* to have pity on

miseria, -ae, *f.,* trouble, woe, distress

misericordia, -ae, *f.,* pity, compassion

mittō, -ere, mīsī, missum, to send

modestia, -ae, *f.,* restraint, discipline; reticence

modestus, -a, -um, *adj.,* restrained, temperate, mild, modest

modicus, -a, -um, *adj.,* restrained, moderate, temperate

modo, *adv.,* just, only; **modo ... modo,** at one time ... at another time

modus, -ī, *m.,* manner, way, limit

mōlior, -īrī, molītus sum, to build up, construct, get under way

mollis, -e, *adj.,* soft

mollitiēs, -ēī, *f.,* softness, luxury, ease

moneō (2), to warn

monitor, -ōris, *m.,* a councilor, preceptor

mons, montis, *m.,* hill, mountain

mora, -ae, *f.,* delay, stay, impediment, obstacle

morbus, -ī, *m.,* disease, illness, sickness

mors, mortis, *f.,* death

mortālis, -is, *m.,* human being, mortal

mōs, mōris, *m.,* customary or traditional way; (*pl.*) morals; **mōs maiōrum,** inherited custom or tradition; convention

moueō, -ēre, mōuī, mōtum, to move; **mouēre senātū,** to remove from the senatorial roll

muliebris, -e, *adj.,* typical of a woman, womanish

mulier, -eris, *f.,* woman; a wife or mistress

multitūdō, -inis, *f.,* host, crowd, throng

multus, -a, -um, *adj.,* numerous, many

Muluccha, -ae, *f.,* the River Muluccha

munditia, -ae, *f.,* cleanliness, manners, refinement of appearance

mūnificentia, -ae, *f.,* bounty, munificence

mūtō (1), to exchange, barter

mūtuus, -a, -um, *adj.,* on loan

nam, *conj.,* for, because; **namque,** *conj.,* certainly, to be sure, yes; for, because

narrō (1), to relate, tell say, describe

nascor, -ī, nātus sum, to be by birth, be born

nātiō, -ōnis, *f.,* people, race, nation

nātūra, -ae, *f.,* nature

nāuis, -is, *f.,* ship

nē, *conj.,* so that not, lest

nē, *particle,* (*Greek*) truly, indeed, assuredly

-ne, *enclitic,* whether if, or

necesse, *adv.,* indispensible, essential, necessary

necessitūdō, -inis, *f.,* what is required, needs, demands

necō (1), to put to death, kill

nefandus, -a, -um, *adj.,* wicked, impious, heinous; unspeakable

neglegō, -ere, neglexī, neglectum, to ignore

negōtior, -ārī, negotiātus sum, to do business, trade

negōtium, -iī, *n.,* work, business; problem

nēmō, -inis, *m.,* no one, nobody

neque, *conj.,* nor, and not; **neque ... neque,** neither ... nor

nī, *conj.,* but for the fact that, if it were not that

nihil, *n. indecl.,* nothing

nihilō minus, *adv.,* none the less, notwithstanding, just the same

nihilum, -ī, *n.,* nothing

nimis, *adv.,* too much

nisi, *conj.,* unless, except, if not

nōbilis, -e, *adj.,* generally known or familiar; renowned, famous; aristocratic

nōbilitās, -tātis, *f.,* nobility of rank or birth

nolō, nolle, noluī, —, to be unwilling, not want to

Nomas, -adis *or* **-ados,** *m.,* nomads, pastoral tribes

nōmen, -inis, *n.,* name

nōminō (1), to mention by name

nōn, *adv.,* not

nōnnullus, -a, -um, *adj.,* not a few; some

nōn sōlum ... sed etiam, *conj.,* not only ... but also

nōs, *pron.,* we

noscō, -ere, nōuī, nōtum, to get to know, ascertain; (*perfect tenses*) to know

noster, -stra, -strum, *poss. pron.,* our, Roman

nouitās, -tātis, *f.,* newness, novelty

nouus, -a, -um, *adj.,* new, novel

nox, noctis, *f.,* night

nūbō, -ere, nupsī, nuptum, + *dat.,* to get married to

nullus, -a, -um, *adj.,* not any, no, none

num, *interr.,* whether by any chance

Numantīnus, -a, -um, *adj.,* of or concerning Numantia

numerus, -ī, *m.,* number

Numida, -ae, *m.,* an inhabitant of Numidia, a Numidian

Numidia, -ae, *f.,* the country of the Numidians

nunc, *adv.,* now

nuntiō (1), to report, announce

nuptiae, -ārum, *f. pl.,* marriage ceremony and festivities, wedding

ob, *prep.* + *acc.,* towards, in front of, on behalf of, on account of

obiciō, -ere, -iēcī, -iectum, to expose to danger

obiectō (1), + *dat.,* to cite as ground for disapproval; to throw in one's teeth

oblongus, -a, -um, *adj.,* elongated

obnoxius, -a, -um, *adj.,* bound, indebted, subservient

obscūrus, -a, -um, *adj.,* little known, insignificant, humble

obsideō, -ēre, -sēdī, -sessum, to besiege, blockade

obtineō, -ēre, -tinuī, -tentum, to be generally believed or acted upon, prevail, obtain

obuiam, *adv.,* in the way or path of; **obuiam īre,** to face up to opposition or danger

occidens, -ntis, *m.,* the west

occidō, -ere, -cidī, -cāsum, to die, be struck down, fall

occultō (1), to conceal, suppress

occultus, -a, -um, *adj.,* hidden from sight, concealed; **in occultō,** in hiding or concealment

occupō (1), to occupy, fill up

occursō (1), to block the path of, obstruct continually

Ōceanus, -ī, *m.,* a sea flowing around the land mass of the known world

oculus, -ī, *m.,* eye

offendō, -ere, -fendī, -fensum, to strike against; to trouble, upset

offerō, -ferre, obtulī, oblātum, to offer, bring to

officiō, -ere, -fēcī, -fectum, to be an obstacle (to someone's plans)

officium, -iī, *n.,* task

omittō, -ere, -mīsī, -missum, to abandon, leave off

omnis, -e, *adj.,* all, every

onerō (1), to load with freight

opera, -ae, *f.,* effort, work; **operam dare,** + *dat.,* to devote one's attention to

opīniō, -ōnis, *f.,* opinion, belief

oportet, oportuit, *impers.,* it is proper, right

oppidum, -ī, *n.,* town

opportūnitās, -tātis, *f.,* advantageousness, convenience

opportūnus, -a, -um, *adj.,* favorable, advantageous, timely

opprimō, -ere, -pressī, -pressum, to overpower, crush, suppress

ops, opis, *f.,* power; (*pl.*) financial resources

optō (1), to wish for, desire

optumus, -a, -um, *superl. adj.,* best

opulenter, *adv.,* richly, sumptuously

opulentus, -a, -um, *adj.,*
wealthy, opulent

opus, -eris, *n.,* work; **opus est,**
+ *dat. of person and abl.,* it is
essential, necessary

ōra, -ae, *f.,* edge, border; **ōra**
maritima, the sea coast

ōrātiō, -ōnis, *f.,* speech, formal
address

orbis, -is, *m.,* sphere, globe;
orbis terrae, the world

Orestilla, -ae, *f.,* Orestilla

orīgō, -inis, *f.,* beginning, start,
origin, descent

orior, -īrī, ortus sum, to arise

ōrō (1), to beg, beseech

ortus, -ūs, *m.,* rising; **solis**
ortus, the east

ostendō, -ere, ostendī,
ostentum, to show

ostentātiō, -ōnis, *f.,* exhibition,
display

ostentō (1), to display, exhibit

ōtium, -iī, *n.,* spare time,
leisure

P., Publius

pābulum, -i, *n.,* fodder, food

paeniteō, -ēre, -uī, —, + *gen.,* to
feel regret

pālor, -ārī, palātus sum, to
wander

pār, paris, *adj.,* similar, equal,
matching in qualities

parcō, -ere, pepercī, parsum, +
dat., to spare, refrain from

pārens, -ntis, *m./f.,* parent; (*pl.*)
ancestors

pāreō, -ēre, -uī, —, + *dat.,* to obey

pariō, -ere, peperī, partum, to
bring forth, produce, give
rise to; to procure, get

pariter, *adv.,* evenly, equally

parō (1), to make ready for
action, prepare

pars, partis, *f.,* portion, part;
political party or faction

partim, *adv.,* in part, partly

parum, *adv.,* too little, not
enough

paruus, -a, -um, *adj.,* small

passim, *adv.,* here and there, all
over the place, at random

pater, -tris, *m.,* father, senator

patera, -ae, *f.,* shallow bowl or
dish used in libations

patiens, -ntis, *adj.,* patient,
enduring

patior, patī, passus sum, to
suffer, bear, put up with,
tolerate; to leave in such a
condition

patrō (1), to bring to
completion, accomplish

patrōcinium, -iī, *n.,* defense or
protection, patronage

paucī, -ae, -a, *adj. pl.,* few

paucitās, -tātis, *f.,* fewness,
scantiness

paulātim, *adv.,* little by little

paulō, *adv.,* by only a small
amount, by a little,
somewhat

paululum, *adv.,* only to a small
extent, little

paulum, *adv.,* only to a small
extent, little

paupertās, -tātis, *f.,* poverty

pax, pācis, *f.,* peace

pecūnia, -ae, *f.,* money

pecus, -oris, *n.,* livestock, farm animal

pedes, -itis, *m.,* footsoldier; *(pl.)* infantry

pendō, -ere, pependī, pensum, to weigh; **nihil pensi habēre,** to have no scruples; to regard as of no importance

penes, *prep.* + *acc.,* in the hands of, to the hands of

pēnūria, -ae, *f.,* scarcity, want

per, *prep.* + *acc.,* through, along, during, by means of, for, by

percontor, -ārī, percontātus sum, to investigate

perdūcō, -ere, -dūxī, -ductum, to conduct, bring

perfugium, -iī, *n.,* refuge, shelter, sanctuary

perīculum, -ī, *n.,* danger

permisceō, -ēre, -miscuī, -mixtum, to mix

permittō, -ere, -mīsī, -missum, to allow, permit

permoueō, -ēre, -mōuī, -mōtum, to excite, upset

perniciēs, -ēī, *f.,* destruction, injury, bane

Persa, -ae, *m.,* a native of Persia, Persian

perscrībō, -ere, -scripsī, -scriptum, to write a detailed record of

perterreō (2), to frighten greatly, terrify

perturbō (1), to throw into confusion; to upset

perueniō, -īre, -uēnī, -uentum, to arrive at

pessumus, -a, -um, *superl. adj.,* worst

petō, -ere, -īuī, -ītum, to attack; to aim at; to seek, strive after

Petreius, -ī, *m.,* Petreius

phalerae, -ārum, *f. pl.,* military decoration, medal worn on the breastplate

Philaenī, -ōrum, *m. pl.,* Philaeni, two Carthaginian brothers

Phoenix, -īcis, *m.,* a Phoenician

pictus, -a, -um, *adj.,* embroidered in color

pīlum, -ī, *n.,* javelin

placeō (2), + *dat.,* to be pleasing, acceptable

plebs, plēbis, *f.,* common people, mob; ordinary citizens

plērumque, *adv.,* generally, often, largely

plērusque, -aque, -umque, *adj.,* most of; most people, the majority, very many

plūrēs, -a, *adj. pl.,* more; most people

plūrumus, -a, -um, *superl. adj.,* the greatest number of, very many

plūs, -ris, *adj.,* more

poena, -ae, *f.,* penalty, punishment; **poenas dare,** to pay the penalty, suffer the punishment

pollens, -ntis, *adj.,* exerting power, strong, potent

polliceor, -ērī, pollitus sum, to promise

polluō, -ere, polluī, pollūtum, to soil, stain; to degrade, violate

pōnō, -ere, posuī, positum, to place, set, put

populāris, -e, *adj.,* popular, of the people

populāris, -is, *m.,* fellow citizen; associate, accomplice

populus, -ī, *m.,* people

Porcius, -iī, *m.,* Porcius

portō (1), to carry

poscō, -ere, poposcī, —, to ask for, demand, call for

possideō, -ēre, -sēdī, -sessum, to have in one's control, hold, occupy

possum, posse, potuī, —, to be able

post, *prep.* + *acc.,* after

post, *adv.,* after

posteā, *adv.,* subsequently, afterwards

posterī, -ōrum, *m. pl.,* descendants

posterius, *compar. adv.,* at a later time

postquam, *conj.,* after

postrēmō, *adv.,* finally, lastly

postulō (1), to ask for, demand, require

potentia, -ae, *f.,* power, influence

potestās, -tātis, *f.,* power, command, control

pōtō (1), to drink to excess, get drunk

praeceps, *adv.,* headlong

praeceptum, -ī, *n.,* teaching, instruction, precept

praecipiō, -ere, -cēpī, -ceptum, to take before; to give as a command, order

praeclārus, -a, -um, *adj.,* outstandingly bright, brilliant, glorious

praeda, -ae, *f.,* booty

praedīcō, (1), to proclaim to be, describe as

praeficiō, -ere, -fēcī, -fectum, to put in charge of, set over

praemittō, -ere, -mīsī, -missum, to send in advance

praemium, -iī, *n.,* reward

praeposterus, -a, -um, *adj.,* wrong-headed

praesens, -ntis, *adj.,* present, being present

praesidium, -iī, *n.,* defense, protection, garrison, fort

praeter, *prep.* + *acc.,* beyond, besides, other than

praetereā, *adv.,* in addition to that, as well, besides

praetereō, -īre, -iī *or* **-īuī, -itum,** to pass over

praetōrius, -a, -um, *adj.,* belonging to a commander; **cohors praetoria,** a general's bodyguard

praetūra, -ae, *f.,* office of praetor, praetorship

prāuus, -a, -um, *adj.,* corrupt, debased

pretium, -iī, *n.,* value, worth, price

prīmus, -a, -um, *adj.,* first,
uttermost, extreme, earliest,
best

princeps, -ipis, *m.,* chief, head,
leader

pristinus, -a, -um, *adj.,* antique,
ancient; former, previous

prīuātim, *adv.,* in a private
capacity, privately

prīuātus, -a, -um, *adj.,* private,
unofficial

prīuignus, -ī, *m.,* stepson

prius, *compar. adv.,* before,
earlier; in advance, first

priusquam, *conj.,* before

prō, *prep. + abl.,* before, in front
of, on behalf of, in place of;
in proportion to; **pro certo,**
as or for a certainty

probrum, -ī, *n.,* scandal,
misdeed, offense, fault

probus, -a, -um, *adj.,* righteous,
morally excellent

procax, -ācis, *adj.,* lively,
skittish, frivolous

prōcēdō, -ere, -cessī, -cessum,
to make progress, succeed;
to progress, advance spread;
to benefit

procul, *adv.,* away, apart, afar

**prōdō, -ere, prodidī,
proditum,** to betray, forsake

proelium, -iī, *n.,* battle

profectō, *adv.,* undoubtedly,
assuredly

proficiscor, -ī, profectus sum,
to set out

profūsus, -a, -um, *adj.,*
immoderate, extravagant

prohibeō (2), to keep from,
avert, stop, restrain

promptus, -a, -um, *adj.,*
prompt, keen, active, quick

prope, *adv.,* almost, nearly

prope, *prep. + acc.,* near, by

properē, *adv.,* speedily, quickly,
without delay

properō (1), to act with haste,
hurry, be quick

propinquus, -a, -um, *adj.,* near,
close, neighboring

propter, *prep. + acc.,* because of

prorsus, *adv.,* indeed, more
than that, even, in fact

prōsāpia, -ae, *f.,* lineage,
family

prōsum, prodesse, profuī, —,
to be helpful, advantageous,
beneficial

prōuidentia, -ae, *f.,* foresight,
providence

prōuideō, -ēre, -uīdī, -uīsum,
to provide for or against,
see to

prōuincia, -ae, *f.,* province

proxumus, -a, -um, *adj.,*
nearest, closest

psallō, -ere, -ī, —, to play on
the cithara

pūblicē, *adv.,* officially, by or
for the public, publicly

pudīcitia, -ae, *f.,* sexual purity,
chastity, virtue

pudor, pudōris, *m.,* shame,
sense of decency

pueritia, -ae, *f.,* boyhood

pugnō (1), to contend in battle,
fight

puluis, -eris, *m.,* dust
Pūnicus, -a, -um, *adj.,* Punic
putō (1), to think

Q., Quintus
quaerō, -ere, quaesīuī, -sītum,
    to seek; **quaeso** + *imperative,*
    I ask you, please
quaesītus, -a, -um, *adj.,*
    carefully worked out,
    elaborate
quaestor, -ōris, *m.,* one who
    holds the office of quaester
quaestus, -ūs, *m.,* gainful
    employment or occupation;
    profit
quam, *adv.,* how; than
quamquam, *conj.,* although
quamuīs, *conj.,* although
quantum, -ī, *interr. adj.,* how
    much?
quantus, -a, -um, *adj.,* how
    great, how much
quasi, *conj.,* as if
-que, *enclitic conj.,* and
queror, -ī, questus sum,
    to express discontent,
    complain, grumble
questus, -ūs, *m.,* complaint
quī, quae, quod, *rel. pron.,* who,
    which; *at the beginning of a*
    sentence, this, he
quia, *conj.,* because
quīdam, quaedam, quiddam,
    pron., a certain, a certain
    one, somebody
quidem, *adv.,* certainly,
    indeed
quiēs, -ētis, *f.,* repose, rest

quīlubet, quaelubet,
    quodlubet, *indef. pron.,*
    whatever or whichever you
    please
quīn, *conj.,* rather, but; +
    subjunctive, rather that
quippe, *adv.,* indeed why, for
    namely, obviously
Quirītēs, -ītium, *m. pl.,* Quirites,
    citizens of Rome collectively
quis, quid? *interr. pron.,* who?
    what?
quisnam, quaenam, quidnam,
    pron., who or what in the
    world; who or what, pray
quisquam, quicquam, *indef.*
    pron., any, anyone at all
quisque, quaeque, quidque,
    indef. pron., each, each one
quod, *conj.,* because; but
quom. *See* **cum**
quoniam, *conj.,* since

rapīna, -ae, *f.,* plunder, booty
ratiō, -ōnis, *f.,* plan, scheme
redeō, -īre, rediī, reditum, to
    return, go back
referō, -ferre, rettulī, relātum,
    to bring back; to relate,
    report, tell
regiō, -ōnis, *f.,* district, region,
    locality
regnum, -ī, *n.,* kingship,
    political control, tyranny
regō, -ere, rexī, rectum, to rule
regredior, -ī, -gressus sum, to
    return, go back
relicuus, -a, -um, *adj.,* the rest
    of, the remaining

relinquō, -ere, reliquī, relictum, to leave behind, abandon

remedium, -iī, *n.,* remedy, cure

remoueō, -ēre, -mōuī, -mōtum, to remove, banish, do away with

reor, rērī, ratus sum, to think, imagine, suppose, deem

repente, *adv.,* suddenly

reperiō, -īre, repperī, repertum, to find by looking, discover

repetō, -ere, -petīuī, -petītum, to demand or claim back

reputō (1), to think over, reflect on

requiescō, -ere, -quiēuī, -quiētum, to rest, desist from activity

requīrō, -ere, -quisīuī, -quisītum, to ask or inquire about

rēs, reī, *f.,* thing, fact, matter; property; (*pl.*) **rēs gestae,** past deeds, history; **rēs nouae,** revolution

rēs publica, reī publicae, *f.,* affairs of state, public good, body politic, state

resistō, -ere, -stitī, —, to make a stand, offer resistance

respondeō, -ēre, -spondī, -sponsum, to reply, answer

reticeō, -ēre, -ticuī, —, to keep silent

retineō, -ēre, -tinuī, -tentum, to hold fast, cling to, retain

rex, rēgis, *m.,* king

Rōma, -ae, *f.,* Rome

Rōmānus, -a, -um, *adj.,* Roman

rūmor, -ōris, *m.,* common talk, gossip

rursus, *adv.,* backwards, again; on the other hand

sacer, -cra, -crum, *adj.,* sacred, hallowed

sacerdōs, -ōtis, *m.,* priest

saepe, *adv.,* often, frequently

saepenumerō, *adv.,* on many occasions, repeatedly

saeuitia, -ae, *f.,* barbarity, cruelty, violence, ferocity

saeuus, -a, -um, *adj.,* harsh, savage, ferocious

saltō (1), to dance

salūber, salubris, salubre, *adj.,* beneficial to the health, healthy, beneficial

salūtō (1), to greet, call on to pay respects

sanctus, -a, -um, *adj.,* holy, sacred

sānē, *adv.,* soundly, certainly, decidedly

Sanga, -ae, *m.,* Sanga

sanguis, -inis, *m.,* blood

sapientia, -ae, *f.,* wisdom

satis, *adv.,* enough, sufficiently

saucius, -a, -um, *adj.,* wounded

scelestus, -a, -um, *adj.,* guilty, wicked, criminal

scelus, -eris, *n.,* crime, villainy

scēna, -ae, *f.,* stage

scīlicet, *adv.,* naturally, evidently, doubtless

sciō, -īre, -īuī, -ītum, to know

Scīpiō, -ōnis, *m.*, Scipio

scītē, *adv.*, with practical knowledge, savoir-faire

scrībō, -ere, scrīpsī, scrīptum, to write; mīlitēs scrībere, to draft an army

sē, *reflex. pron.*, himself, herself, itself, themselves

secundus, -a, -um, *adj.*, lying in the direction of one's travel; following the sea-coast

secus, *no gen., n.*, sex or its members collectively

sed, *conj.*, but

sedeō, -ēre, sēdī, sessum, to sit, be seated

sēdēs, -is, *f.*, abode, dwelling place

sēditiō, -ōnis, *f.*, violent political discord, rebellion, mutiny

sedō (1), to cause to subside, relieve, calm down

semper, *adv.*, always, all the time

Semprōnia, -ae, *f.*, Sempronia

senātor, -ōris, *m.*, senator

senātus, -ūs *or* -ī, *m.*, senate

senectūs, -tūtis, *f.*, old age

sententia, -ae, *f.*, vote given in an assembly; opinion

sequor, -ī, secūtus sum, to follow, attend upon

sermō, -ōnis, *m.*, talk, speech, conversation

seruīlis, -e, *adj.*, slavish, servile, ignoble

seruitium, -iī, *n.*, slavery, bondage

seuēritās, -tātis, *f.*, sternness, severity, seriousness

sī, *conj.*, if

sīc, *adv.*, thus, so

sīcut, *conj.*, just as

signum, -ī, *n.*, sign for action, signal

silentium, -iī, *n.*, silence

sileō, -ēre, -uī, —, to be silent

simul, *adv.*, together with, jointly, at the same time; simul et, as soon as, at the moment that

simulācrum, -ī, *n.*, image, statue

simulātor, -ōris, *m.*, a pretender, one who puts on pretense

simulō (1), to pretend

sine, *prep. + abl.*, without

singulī, -ae, -a, *adj. pl.*, single, individual

situs, -ūs, *m.*, position, situation; geography

societās, -tātis, *f.*, partnership, alliance

socius, -iī, *m.*, ally

socordia, -ae, *f.*, sluggishness

sōl, sōlis, *m.*, sun

soleō, -ēre, solitus sum, to be accustomed to

sōlitūdō, -inis, *f.*, uninhabited country; (*pl.*) desert, waste

sollemne, -is, *n.*, religious ceremony, ritual observance

sollertia, -ae, *f.*, cleverness, resourcefulness

sollicitō (1), to disturb, harass, worry, vex

sōlus, -a, -um, *adj.,* alone
sordidus, -a, -um, *adj.,* foul, filthy, dirty; lacking refinement, low, vulgar
spargō, -ere, sparsī, sparsum, to sprinkle
spērō (1), to look forward to, hope
spēs, -eī, *f.,* hope
spīrō (1), to breathe
spoliō (1), to strip of equipment
spolium, -iī, *n.,* spoils of war, booty
statuō, -ere, -uī, -ūtum, to decide
status, -ūs, *m.,* position, state, circumstance
stīpendium, -iī, *n.,* pay, payment
strēnuē, *adv.,* with energy or vigor, forcefully
strēnuus, -a, -um, *adj.,* active, vigorous, keen, energetic
strepitus, -ūs, *m.,* noise
studium, -iī, *n.,* zeal, ardor, enthusiasm
stuprum, -ī, *n.,* shame, dishonor; illicit sexual intercourse of any sort, improper relations
sub, *prep.* + *abl.,* under; + *acc.,* subject to
subdolus, -a, -um, *adj.,* sly, deceitful, treacherous
subleuō (1), to raise, lift, lighten, alleviate
subueniō, -īre, -uēnī, -uentum, to come to the support of, provide help for

succurrō, -ere, -currī, -cursum, to run to the rescue of
sūdor, sudōris, *m.,* sweat
Sulla, -ae, *m.,* Sulla
Sullānus, -a, -um, *adj.,* Sullan
sum, esse *or* **fore, fuī, futurus,** to be; to exist
summus, -a, -um, *adj.,* highest, utmost, uppermost
sumō, -ere, sumpsī, sumptum, to take up, take on, adopt; **sumere mutuum,** to borrow
sumptus, -ūs, *m.,* expenditure, expense
super, *prep.* + *acc.,* beyond; further from the coast
superbia, -ae, *f.,* lofty self esteem, haughtiness
superbus, -a, -um, *adj.,* proud, haughty
superō (1), to overcome, surmount, rise above, prevail over, defeat
suppellex, -ectilis, *f.,* furniture
supplementum, -ī, *n.,* reinforcement
supplex, -icis, *adj.,* suppliant, making humble entreaty
supplicium, -iī, *n.,* punishment
supplicō (1), to worship
suprā, *adv.,* above
suscipiō, -ere, -cēpī, -ceptum, to take up, adopt, assume, take on
sustentō (1), to support
sustineō, -ēre, -tinuī, -tentum, to make possible

suus, -a, -um, *poss. pron.,* his, her, its, their [own]

Syrtes, -ium, *f. pl.,* the Syrtes, sandbanks off the coast of Africa

tālis, -e, *adj.,* of such a sort, such

tam, *adv.,* so much, so

tamen, *adv.,* nevertheless

tametsī, *conj.,* even though

tandem, *adv.,* at length, at last, finally

tantummodo, *adv.,* only, merely, only just

tantus, -a, -um, *adj.,* so great, so much

tardus, -a, -um, *adj.,* slow

tectum, -ī, *n.,* roofed building, roof, house

tegō, -ere, texī, tectum, to cover

tēlum, -ī, *n.,* weapon

temeritās, -tātis, *f.,* recklessness, impetuosity

temperō (1), to behave with moderation

tempestās, -tātis, *f.,* time, weather; violent circumstances; storm

templum, -ī, *n.,* temple

temptō (1), to test, examine, try out, make an attempt on

tempus, -oris, *n.,* time

tendō, -ere, tetendī, tentum, to stretch toward; to aim

teneō, -ēre, -uī, —, to hold, keep, occupy

terra, -ae, *f.,* land, earth, ground, soil

terreō (2), to alarm, terrify, frighten

terror, -ōris, *m.,* extreme fear, alarm

tertius, -a, -um, *adj.,* third

Thēraeus, -a, -um, *adj.,* Theran, native to the island of Thera (modern Santorini)

timeō, -ēre, -uī, —, to fear, be afraid

timidus, -a, -um, *adj.,* cowardly, fearful

timor, -ōris, *m.,* fear

toga, -ae, *f.,* toga

tolerō (1), to bear, undergo, endure, tolerate

tollō, -ere, sustulī, sublātum, to raise, remove, eliminate

tonitrus, -ūs, *m.,* thunder

trahō, -ere, traxī, tractum, to drag, draw; to ponder, go on considering

trans, *prep. + acc.,* across or over

transenna, -ae, *f.,* netting, a trap for birds made of netting; rope

transuehō, -ere, -uexī, -uectum, to sail across

transuorsus, -a, -um, *adj.,* carried off one's true proper course, derailed, askew

trepidō (1), to panic, feel apprehensive

triumphus, -ī, *m.,* triumph, honor of a triumphal procession

tuba, -ae, *f.,* trumpet

tueor, -ērī, tuitus sum, to look at, protect

tugurium, -iī, *n.,* hut, shack
Tullius, -iī, *m.,* Tullius
tum, *adv.,* then, at that moment
turpis, -e, *adj.,* foul, shameful
tūs, tūris, *n.,* frankincense; incense
tūtē, *adv.,* safely
tūtor, -ārī, tutātus sum, to watch over; to preserve unimpaired, maintain; to protect or defend
tūtus, -a, -um, *adj.,* safe, secure

uacuus, -a, -um, *adj.,* empty
uagus, -a, -um, *adj.,* wandering
ualidus, -a, -um, *adj.,* robust, strong, powerful
uānitās, -tātis, *f.,* emptiness
Vargunteius, -ī, *m.,* Vargunteius
uariē, *adv.,* variously, in different ways
uarius, -a, -um, *adj.,* multifarious, varied, changeable
uastō (1), to plunder, ravage, lay waste
ubi, *conj.,* where, in what place
uēcordia, -ae, *f.,* frenzy
uehementer, *adv.,* with great force, energetically, with vigor
uel, *conj.,* or; **uel . . . uel,** either . . . or
uēlox, -ōcis, *adj.,* swift, speedy, rapid
ueniō, -īre, uēnī, uentum, to come
uēnor, -ārī, uenātus sum, to go hunting, hunt

uenter, -tris, *m.,* belly
uerbum, -ī, *n.,* word; (*pl.*) talk, mere words
uērē, *adv.,* really, truly, correctly, exactly, truthfully
uērō, *adv.,* certainly, indeed; however, yet
uersus, -ūs, *m.,* a line of poetry
uērum, *conj.,* but, on the other hand, however
Vesta, -ae, *f.,* Roman goddess of the domestic hearth
ueterānus, -a, -um, *adj.,* having experience, veteran
uetus, -eris, *adj.,* old
uexillum, -ī, *n.,* military standard, banner with fringe hung from a cross bar or lance
uexō (1), to attack constantly, afflict, harass
uia, -ae, *f.,* road
uictor, uictōris, *m.,* victor
uictōria, -ae, *f.,* victory; Victory (personified)
uideō, -ēre, uīdī, uīsum, to see
uideor, -ērī, uīsus sum, to seem
uigeō, -ēre, -uī, —, to be successful, thrive, flourish
uigilia, -ae, *f.,* patrol, guard, watch
uigilō (1), to stay awake, be watchful
uīlicus, -ī, *m.,* overseer, manager
uincō, -ere, uīcī, uictum, to conquer
uīnum, -ī, *n.,* wine
uiolentia, -ae, *f.,* unreasonable use of force; violence

uir, uirī, *m.,* man, husband

uirgō, -inis, *f.,* virgin

uirīlis, -e, *adj.,* male, manly, masculine

uirtūs, -tūtis, *f.,* excellence of character, goodness, prowess

uīs, uis, *f.,* physical strength, force, violence

uīsō, -ere, uīsī, —, to go and look at; to call on, go and see

uīta, -ae, *f.,* life

uitium, -iī, *n.,* moral failing, vice

uīuō, -ere, uixī, uictum, to live one's life

uīuus, -a, -um, *adj.,* alive, living

ullus, -a, -um, *adj.,* any, any at all

ulterior, -us, *compar. adj.,* farther away, more distant

ultrā, *adv.,* on the far side, farther off, beyond

Vmbrenus, -ī, *m.,* Umbrenus

umquam, *adv.,* at any time, ever

undique, *adv.,* from all sides, from every side

ūniuersus, -a, -um, *adj.,* all without exception, entire

ūnus, -a, -um, *adj.,* one, a single

uocō (1), to call

uolgus, -ī, *n.,* common people, crowd

uolnerō (1), to inflict a wound

uolnus, -neris, *n.,* wound

uolō, uelle, uoluī, —, to wish, want

uoltus, -ūs, *m.,* countenance, face

uolucris, -cris, *f.,* bird

uoluntās, -tātis, *f.,* disposition, will, wish

uoluō, -ere, uoluī, uolūtum, to turn over; to turn over in the mind

uoluptās, -tātis, *f.,* pleasure, delight

uorsō (1), to busy or concern oneself in an activity, be involved in

uorsus, *prep.* + *acc.,* in the direction of, towards (following geographical names)

uorsus, *adv.,* in a specified direction, towards

uortō, -ere, uortī, uorsum, to turn, change

uōs, *pron.,* you (*pl.*)

uoster, -tra, -trum, *poss. pron.,* your (*pl.*)

urbānus, -a, -um, *adj.,* pertaining to the city, urban

Vrbinus, -ī, *m.,* Urbinus

urbs, urbis, *f.,* city

usque (ad), *adv.,* all the way to, right up to, as far as

ūsus, -ūs, *m.,* use, experience

ut, *conj.,* as, when; + *subjunctive,* so that, with the result that

uterque, utraque, utrumque, *pron.,* each of the two

utī. *See* **ut**

ūtilis, -e, *adj.,* useful

ūtor, ūtī, ūsus sum, + *abl.,* to use, make use of

utrimque, *adv.,* on both sides